The BISTO *Book of*
Meat Cookery

The BISTO Book of
Meat Cookery

Sonia Allison

David & Charles
Newton Abbot　London　North Pomfret (Vt)

Also by Sonia Allison

The Book of Microwave Cookery
Sonia Allison's Book of Preserving

Drawings by Andrew Harrison
Colour plates by RHM Foods Ltd

British Library Cataloguing in Publication Data
Allison, Sonia
  The Bisto book of meat cookery.
  1. Cookery (Meat)
  I. Title
  641.6'6   TX749

  ISBN 0-7153-7893-7

Printed in Great Britain
by Ebenezer Baylis and Son Limited
The Trinity Press, Worcester
for David & Charles (Publishers) Limited
Brunel House Newton Abbot Devon

Published in the United States of America
by David & Charles Inc
North Pomfret Vermont 05053 USA

In association with RHM Foods Ltd

Contents

Introduction

Meat is here to stay, and if there has been a slight shift away from the traditional weekend roast and we are placing greater emphasis on mince, chicken and the less expensive cuts of meat, then this book has something in it for everyone.

It is filled with an assortment of world-wide recipes ranging in character from exotic and luxurious curries, Stroganovs, kebabs and family joints (some of us still, after all, *do* buy them!) to more basic but delicious hamburgers, scotch broth, toad-in-the-hole, liver or kidneys. Also included, from the Bisto kitchens, is a comprehensive guide to the different cuts of meat and which to choose for specific dishes; useful carving instructions; suggested accompaniments for beef, lamb, pork, chicken, turkey, duck and goose; and hints on freezing meat.

When the idea of this book was first mooted, I decided there and then against making it a 'teach-in' on meat cookery. It seemed more practical to produce an anthology of appetising and appealing recipes for all to enjoy, without too much technical jargon to spoil the fun! Thus I am indebted to all my friends at Bisto for letting me have my own way, and to all my overseas contacts for providing dishes suitable for adaptation.

SONIA ALLISON
HERTFORDSHIRE, 1980

Note

The recipes in this book are given in both metric and imperial measures, so use which you please. But remember that the results may not be exactly identical as it is impossible to translate one set of measures into the other without making very slight adjustments. Also, do not combine some metric with some imperial measures as results will suffer.

1 Beef and Beef Dishes

Although the price of beef seems particularly high nowadays, we must not forget the wide variety of cuts, many of which do not have wasteful bones or fat; pound for £1 beef remains the best value for money. We all know how to cook the more expensive cuts, but it is the clever cook who knows how to make a good meal from the cheaper cuts. For example, back and top ribs make excellent slow roasting joints. It is well worth getting to know the cuts of beef.

Choosing and Buying Beef

Look for a fresh, slightly moist appearance, as the redness of the beef varies after cutting due to exposure to air. Prime cuts should look smooth and velvety in texture; economical cuts will have a coarser texture. The fat surrounding the meat should be firm and creamy-white: the colour may vary but should not affect the eating qualities. 'Marbling', the flecks of fat in the meat, aids cooking by helping to keep the meat moist and to retain the flavour.

Some cuts of beef can be 'salted': silverside and brisket, for example, are ideal cuts for this. Salting turns the meat grey in colour, but it goes pink during cooking.

Storing Beef

All cuts of beef should be placed on a plate and lightly covered to prevent drying out. Put in the refrigerator, near the freezing compartment, where the meat will keep for up to three days. Remove the beef from the refrigerator some time before you cook it, so that you can start the cooking at room temperature and obtain the full flavour.

Cuts of Beef

Leg and shin

Coarse in texture: the cheapest kind of stewing steak, suitable for long slow cooking for stews and casseroles. Prime cuts from leg and shin are a very good buy.

Clod and sticking

These are cuts from the neck of beef, and are also sold as cheaper stewing steak. Less coarse in texture than leg and shin, they are suitable for casseroles, hotpots and stews.

Hind and fore-quarter flank

A cut used by our grandparents, and a very economical cut sold on the bone for pot-roasting; or it can be salted.

Jacob's Ladder

A fore-quarter cut, very economical but only cut by some butchers. It comes from the top of the ribs and is very good for pot-roasting.

Brisket

Often sold boneless, but it is much cheaper on the bone and has much more flavour and goodness this way. It carries quite a lot of fat and needs long, slow, moist cooking. This joint can also be bought salted and used for pressed brisket of beef.

Skirt

'Goose skirt' comes from the hind-quarter and is suitable for pies and casseroles. 'Rump skirt' comes from the side of the rump and can be used for frying.

Chuck steak

Good quality lean meat, sold for braising and casseroles. Coming from the fore-quarter, rolled chuck steak can be used as a pot-roasting joint.

Feather blade

Feather blade is the beginning of the blade bone cut across to give pieces of steak in a 'feather' shape with 'feather' markings. It is lean and tender for frying. The trade regard this as a delicacy and you may have to ask your butcher to keep some for you.

Fore-rib

The whole fore-rib consists of four bones and is the traditional British roasting joint. You can buy these as single or double ribs on the bone. If bought as a boneless joint, fore-rib should not be confused with sirloin, which it may resemble.

Top ribs

A fore-quarter cut, usually sold boneless but may also be sold on the bone. The prime cut is known as 'the thick end of top ribs'; it is a lean, economical cut suitable for slow roasting.

Back ribs
Sold on the bone: the centre eye of the back rib is a superb frying steak; the remainder can be rolled and used for pot-roasting or braising.

Aitchbone
A whole joint on the bone weighs about 12 to 14 lb (6 to 7kg), but nowadays it is boned and rolled and sold as a medium-priced hind-quarter roasting joint.

Silverside
Silverside can be bought salted, and is the traditional joint for 'boiled beef and carrots'. There are two cuts of silverside: the number one cut is the prime round cut suitable for roasting, and the number two cut, which is often salted, is frequently presented by the shop as a flash-fry steak.

Top rump or thick flank
The middle cut is the prime one, a good lean joint for roasting. The remaining end pieces are ideal for braising.

Topside or buttock steak
This is sold as two cuts: the 'corner' is the better and commands a higher price. The remainder is cheaper and is suitable for roasting.

Rump steak
Although not as tender as fillet, rump has more flavour and is suitable for frying or grilling. Try to make sure that you get your cut from as near the middle as possible, the most succulent part of the rump.

Fillet steak or tenderloin
This is the tenderest steak and is used for grilling. It runs from the rump to the loin of beef, and its tenderness is its prime virtue.

Sirloin
Sirloin comes in two prime cuts. The number one cut is where the fillet ends. This is the part used for T-bone steaks and is the prime beef cut. The number two cut can be boned and rolled and presented as rolled sirloin.

Wing end
Wing end of the sirloin is slightly cheaper. Sold on or off the bone, this also is a prime roasting joint.

Carving Beef

Carving is like every other job you do—you need the right tools to do it well. You need a good long, sharp carving knife and a two-pronged carving fork with a thumb guard to make sure that the only thing you carve is the meat you mean to cut. No knife stays sharp for ever, so make sure you can keep your carving knife as sharp as it should be: a butcher's steel is the best way to make sure of this.

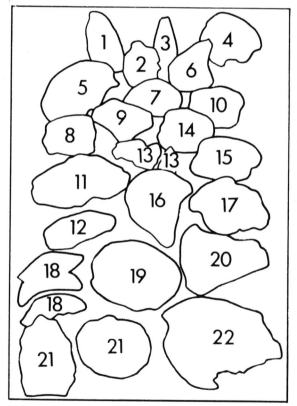

The cuts of beef:
1 *brisket* **2** *aitchbone* **3** *flank* **4** *T-bone end of sirloin* **5** *fore-rib* **6** *wing end of sirloin* **7** *topside (no 2 cut)* **8** *top rib* **9** *Jacob's ladder* **10** *top rump* **11** *chuck steak* **12** *bladebone steak* **13** *fillet steak* **14** *back rib* **15** *silverside* **16** *rump steak* **17** *clod* **18** *feather blade* **19** *leg of beef* **20** *gooseskirt* **21** *shin* **22** *sticking*

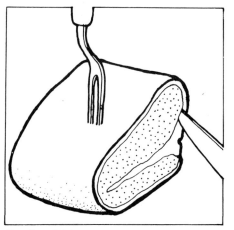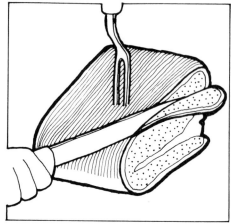

Carving sirloin: loosen the meat from the bone, then cut slices down to the bone

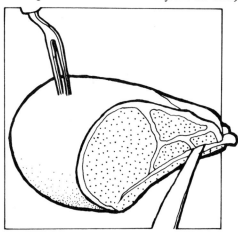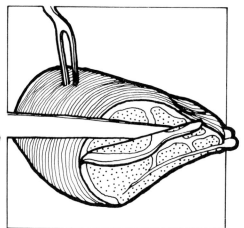

Carving rib: remove the chine bone, then carve downwards

Boned or rolled joints of beef give you no problems. You can carve them either horizontally or vertically: slices should be thin and for preference cut against the grain to make them tenderer. This way, too, you will leave the joint tidier for next time's use when you'll be carving it cold or using it for another recipe.

Sirloin of beef
Before you start carving sirloin, you can make your life easier by loosening the meat from the bone with the carving knife. Slip the knife into the joint close to the bones and follow the bone contour round until the top half of the joint is free. Then carve in slices down to the bone until it is all exposed. Now you can remove the bone and carve the remaining meat which is underneath.

Wing rib of beef
Start at the thick end of the joint by removing the chine bone. Then loosen the narrow ribs. Now the joint is ready for you to carve vertically down in thin slices. Detach the slices from the rib bones and serve.

Roast Beef

Choose your joint for roasting, referring to the list of cuts above. Roast for 20 minutes per pound (500g) plus 20 minutes extra, at 400°F (200°C), Gas 6. Accompany with roast potatoes, green vegetables, horseradish sauce, Yorkshire pudding and Bisto gravy.

In general the amounts to allow per person are:

8 to 12 oz (225 to 350g) beef with bone
4 to 6 oz (125 to 175g) beef without bone

Freezing
Pieces of cooked beef, or made-up beef dishes, may be frozen for up to six months. See the note on freezing on page 119.

Salt Beef

Pickling Brine
How to prepare salted beef for oneself is something I am frequently asked, and below are two brine recipes (one dry and the other wet), followed by recipes for cooking the salt beef itself.

Wet pickle (for about 4lb or 2kg brisket or silverside)
12 to 16oz (350 to 450g) coarse salt (depending on how salty you like your meat)
8pt (4½ litres) water
4oz (125g) demerara sugar
¾oz (20g) saltpetre (available from chemists and added to give the meat its typical redness)
bouquet garni (optional)

1 Put all ingredients into pan. Bring to boil. Lower heat. Simmer ¼ hour. Strain. Cool completely.
2 Place meat in deepish bowl. *Cover* with cold brine. Leave to stand, covered, in the cool, for 2 to 3 days.
3 To ensure even brining, turn the meat over every day.

Dry pickle (for about 4lb or 2kg brisket or silverside)
This is more complicated than the wet pickle but in case you find it more convenient, here is the recipe.

12 to 16oz (350 to 450g) coarse salt (depending on how salty you like your meat to be)
2oz (50g) soft brown sugar
½oz (15g) saltpetre
about ½ level tsp white pepper

1 Rub a good handful of salt well into the meat. Place in a deep bowl. Cover. Leave in the cool for 24 hours.
2 Put remaining ingredients into blender goblet. Run machine at high speed till mixture looks like powder.
3 Rub, bit by bit, into the meat over a period of 7 days. Leave in the cool, turn meat every day and keep the dish covered.

Boiled Brisket or Silverside (serves 6 to 8)
4lb (2kg) salted brisket or silverside, well-washed
cold water
1 heaped tbsp mixed pickling spice
2 medium onions, peeled but left whole
2 medium garlic cloves, peeled but left whole (optional)
2 medium carrots, peeled and cut lengthwise, into 4 strips
2 medium celery stalks, snapped in half

1 Put meat into large pan. Cover with cold water. Soak 2 hours. Change water. Re-cover with fresh water.
2 Bring to boil. Drain. Cover with more fresh water. Add pickling spice and vegetables.
3 Bring to boil again. Skim. Lower heat. Cover. Simmer gently, allowing 30 minutes per pound (500g) and 30 minutes over.
4 Remove from water. Drain. Stand on carving board. Cut into slices and serve with vegetables from pan plus boiled potatoes and suet dumplings (recipe on page 116).

For Jewish-style salt beef, accompany with potato pancakes (page 116) and pickled cucumbers.

Roast Salted Silverside (serves 6 to 8)
Soak and boil beef with vegetables as directed in recipe for boiled brisket or silverside. Drain after ½ hour. Stand meat in casserole or roasting tin and surround with vegetables. Add a bouquet garni if you wish but *not* the loose pickling spice. Cover closely with lid or foil. Cook 3½ hours in a cool oven set to 300°F (150°C), Gas 2. Remove from dish or tin, carve fairly thickly and serve with the boiled vegetables, mashed swedes and creamed potatoes.

Cold Salted Silverside
Any left-overs make an excellent cold meal. Simply wrap in cling film and refrigerate till ready to serve. Slice thinly. Serve with salad, chutney and bread and butter.

Boiled Unsalted Brisket or Silverside (serves 6 to 8)
Follow recipe for boiled brisket or silverside but omit pickling spice. *Do not* boil up and change water. Cover meat and vegetables with cold water. Bring to boil. Skim. Add 3 to 4 level tsp salt. Lower heat. Cover. Simmer slowly until cooked, allowing 30 minutes per pound (500g) and 30 minutes over. Serve with the vegetables with which the meat was cooking and with suet dumplings (page 116).

Steak and kidney pie

Traditional Steak Pie (serves 4 to 6)

1½lb (750g) chuck steak, blade bone, feather blade or
　skirt
1 level tbsp flour mixed with 3 heaped tsp Bisto
2 medium onions, chopped
salt and pepper to taste
¼pt (150ml) water
about 12oz (350g) ready-prepared puff pastry or 8oz
　(225g) shortcrust pastry (homemade or mix)
beaten egg for brushing

1　Cut meat into small cubes. Toss in flour and Bisto
mixture.
2　Fill a 1pt (¾ litre) oval or round pie dish (with rim)
with alternate layers of beef and onions, sprinkling
salt and pepper between layers.
3　Pour water into dish over meat and onions. Roll
out pastry according to type (puff is usually left
thicker than shortcrust).
4　From it cut a lid, 1 inch (2½cm) larger all the way
round than top of dish. Dampen rim with water. Line
with pastry trimmings.
5　Dampen pastry lining strips, then cover with
pastry lid. Press edges well together to seal, then press
into flutes between finger and thumb.
6　Make 2 slits in the lid to allow steam to escape.
Brush with egg. Bake ¼ hour in hot oven set to
450°F (230°C), Gas 8. Reduce temperature to 350°F
(180°C), Gas 4.
7　Continue to bake a further 2 hours, covering pastry
with a piece of foil for the last hour to prevent it
browning too much. Serve hot with vegetables.

Traditional Steak and Kidney Pie (serves 4 to 6)
Follow recipe for traditional steak pie but use 1¼lb
(about 600g) meat and 4oz (125g) cubed ox kidney.

Traditional Steak and Mushroom Pie (serves 4 to 6)
Follow recipe for traditional steak pie but use 1¼lb
(about 600g) meat and 6oz (175g) sliced mushrooms.

Mrs Clancy's Vermont Beefsteak Pie (serves 6)

This is an excellent-tasting pie, adapted from a recipe
given to me in America by Ernestine Clancy, one of
New England's most able and best-known cooks.

1lb (500g) bladebone steak
1oz (25g) bacon dripping or margarine
4 medium carrots, thinly sliced diagonally
2 medium celery stalks, thinly sliced
1 large garlic clove, crushed
1 large onion, thinly sliced
¼pt (150ml) plus 6 tbsp water
¼pt (150ml) dry red wine
salt and pepper to taste
½ level tsp thyme
½ level tsp marjoram
1 level tbsp tomato purée
1 medium bay leaf
1 level tbsp cornflour
3 heaped tsp Bisto
shortcrust pastry made with 8oz (225g) flour and 4oz
　(125g) fat

Roast beef—here a piece of fore-rib

Glaze
1 egg yolk
2 tbsp single cream

1 Cut beef into small cubes. Fry in the dripping or margarine until pieces are well-browned all over. Add carrots, celery, garlic, onion, ¼pt (150ml) water, red wine, salt and pepper to taste, herbs, purée and bay leaf.
2 Bring to the boil. Lower heat and cover pan. Simmer about 1½ hours or until meat is tender.
3 To thicken, mix cornflour and Bisto smoothly with the 6 tbsp water. Pour into beef mixture. Cook, stirring, till thickened. Leave to bubble gently for about 2 minutes. Remove bay leaf. Cool completely.
4 Transfer mixture into large but shallow pie dish with rim. Dampen rim with water. Line with strips of pastry. Cover with rest of pastry, rolled into a lid and also dampened with water round the edges.
5 Pinch all the way round between finger and thumb to seal, then brush top with egg yolk mixed with cream.
6 Bake about 30 to 35 minutes in oven preheated to 375°F (190°C), Gas 5, or until pastry is golden-brown and crisp.

Serve hot with green vegetables to taste and creamed potatoes.

Vermont Beefsteak Pie with Beans

After beef mixture has thickened, stir in about 6oz (175g) cooked green beans. Leave until completely cold before using.

Sea Pie (serves 4)

An old-fashioned stew, topped with a 'lid' of suet pastry.

1½lb (750g) beef shin, diced
2 level tsp cornflour mixed with 3 rounded tsp Bisto
2oz (50g) butter or margarine
4oz (125g) onion, chopped
6oz (175g) mixed root vegetables, diced
½pt (275ml) water
salt and pepper to taste
suet pastry, as in suet dumpling recipe (page 116)

1 Toss meat in mixture of cornflour and Bisto. Fry till well-sealed and brown in the butter or margarine. Remove to a plate temporarily.
2 Add onions to pan. Fry till golden. Stir in rest of vegetables. Fry, uncovered, ¼ hour. Replace meat. Pour water into pan.
3 Bring to boil, stirring. Season. Lower heat. Cover. Simmer slowly 1¾ to 2 hours or until meat is just tender. Stir occasionally.
4 Roll out suet mixture into a round a little smaller than the top of the pan. Stand on top of meat. Cover with lid. Cook ½ hour.

Cut pastry into 4 pieces and serve with the stew.

Steak and Mushroom Plate Pie (serves 4 to 6)

This pie has a top and bottom crust and is made with a filling of *cold* cooked meat and vegetables—rather like a stew sandwich!

1½lb (750g) chuck or bladebone steak
1 level tbsp flour, mixed with 3 heaped tsp Bisto
1oz (25g) lard, margarine or dripping
1 large onion, chopped
4oz (100 to 125g) trimmed mushrooms, peeled and sliced (use stalks as well)
½pt (275ml) water
shortcrust pastry made with 8oz (225g) flour and 4oz (125g) fat (or use 12oz or 350g shortcrust pastry mix)
beaten egg for brushing

1 Cube steak. Coat with flour and Bisto mixture. Heat fat in heavy-based pan.
2 Add onion. Fry over medium heat till golden brown. Add meat to pan. Fry briskly 5 minutes or till pieces are well-sealed and brown.
3 Stir in mushrooms and water. Bring slowly to boil. Lower heat. Cover. Simmer 1½ to 2 hours or until meat is tender. Stir occasionally to prevent sticking and add a little extra water if gravy thickens too much. Leave until completely cold.
4 To complete pie, roll out a little under half the pastry. Use to line a lightly-greased, 8 inch (20cm) heatproof plate or a 7 inch (17½cm) deep enamel plate with rim.
5 Pile filling over pastry, doming it up in the centre so that it supports the crust.
6 Moisten edges with water. Cover with lid rolled from rest of pastry and press edges well together to ensure a secure seal. Press into flutes between finger and thumb or press into ridges with prongs of fork.
7 Make 2 slits in the top to allow steam to escape, then brush lid with beaten egg. Decorate with leaves cut from pastry trimmings and brush with more egg.
8 Stand pie on baking tray and bake 25 to 30 minutes in hot oven set to 425°F (220°C), Gas 7.

Cut into wedges and serve hot with vegetables to taste.

Steak Plate Pie (serves 4 to 6)
Follow recipe for steak and mushroom plate pie but use steak and onion only, and omit mushrooms.

Steak and Kidney Plate Pie (serves 4 to 6)
Follow recipe for steak and mushroom plate pie but use 1¼lb (about 600g) steak and 4oz (100 to 125g) ox kidney, well-washed and cut into small cubes. Omit mushrooms.

Steak and kidney pudding

Steak, Kidney and Mushroom Plate Pie (serves 4 to 6)

Follow recipe for steak and mushroom plate pie but use 1lb (500g) steak, 4oz (100 to 125g) ox kidney and 4oz (100 to 125g) button mushrooms, thickly sliced.

Liver and Bacon Plate Pie (serves 4 to 6)

Follow recipe for steak and mushroom plate pie but use 1lb (500g) cubed ox liver, 4oz (100 to 125g) coarsely chopped unsmoked bacon and the onion. Add 2oz (50g) sliced mushrooms if liked. Simmer filling for ¾ to 1 hour or till liver is cooked through and tender.

Steak and Kidney Pudding (serves 4 to 6)

Suet Pastry
8oz (225g) self-raising flour
1 level tsp salt
4oz (100 to 125g) finely shreaded suet
about 8 tbsp cold water to mix

Filling
12oz (350g) beef skirt or shin, cut into 1 inch (2½cm) cubes
6oz (175g) ox kidney, cut into ½ inch (1¼cm) cubes
1 level tbsp plain flour
4 rounded tsp Onion Bisto
water

1 For pastry, sift flour and salt into a bowl. Toss in suet. Mix to soft dough with water. Knead quickly until smooth, on floured surface.

2 Roll out two-thirds of the pastry and use to line a 2pt (1¼ litre) greased pudding basin. Make sure pastry is pressed well against the sides to prevent 'creases'.

3 Place meat and kidney into mixing bowl. Add flour and Bisto. Toss thoroughly. Spoon into pastry-lined basin.

4 Half-fill basin with water. Dampen edges of pastry. Cover with lid rolled from rest of pastry. Pinch edges of lining pastry and lid well together to seal.

5 Cover with large round of greased greaseproof paper, then overwrap with a double thickness of foil. Tie round basin with string so that the covering stays securely in place.

6 Stand basin in heavy-based pan. Add sufficient boiling water to come halfway up the sides of the basin.

7 Cover with lid and boil gently for 4 hours, topping up pan with boiling water every now and then to keep the water more-or-less the same level all the time the pudding is cooking.

8 Just before serving, remove basin from pan and wipe dry with a cloth. Stand on a plate and tie a clean table napkin round the sides. Spoon portions out on to warm plates.

Serve with boiled potatoes and green vegetables.

Tip

It is not usual for a steak and kidney pudding to be turned out of the basin as is customary with other steamed puddings.

Steak and Mushroom Pudding (serves 4 to 6)

Follow recipe for steak and kidney pudding, but substitute sliced mushrooms for kidneys.

Old English Steak, Kidney and Oyster Pudding (serves 4 to 6)

Follow recipe for steak and kidney pudding, but include 12 shelled oysters in the filling.

Old-Fashioned Steak and Kidney Casserole (serves 6)

1½lb (750g) beef shin, cut into 1 inch (2½cm) cubes
4oz (100 to 125g) ox kidney, cut into small cubes
2 level tbsp flour
2oz (50g) butter or margarine
5 rounded tsp Onion Bisto
1¼pt (¾ litre) water
1 rounded tsp mixed herbs
salt and pepper to taste
4oz (100 to 125g) mussels (either brined in a jar or
   loose from the fishmongers)

1 Toss meat and kidney in the flour. Heat butter or margarine in pan. Add meat and kidney. Fry fairly briskly until well-browned all over.

2 Mix Onion Bisto to smooth paste with some of the water. Blend in rest of water and herbs. Season to taste.

3 Transfer meat and kidney to casserole. Add Bisto and herb liquid. Cover. Cook for 2 hours at 325°F (160°C), Gas 3.

4 Stir in mussels. Cover casserole again. Cook a further ¼ hour.

Serve with creamed potatoes and brussels sprouts.

Four from One: Chili Beef, Exotic Beef, Beef Madras, Paprika Cream Beef

For those occasions when you want to have a 'cook-in' and prepare a selection of tasty dishes for the freezer, I've worked out one basic beef recipe to cook in bulk, and then dressed it up in four different ways.

Basic Beef Stew

8oz (225g) margarine or dripping
8lb (4kg) bladebone or chuck steak, cut into 1 inch
   (2½cm) cubes
2lb (1kg) frozen vegetable stewpack
12 heaped tsp Onion Bisto
2pt (1¼ litre) water
salt and pepper to taste

1 Heat margarine or dripping in large and heavy-based saucepan.

2 Add meat cubes. Fry fairly briskly until well-browned all over, turning frequently.

3 Tip in vegetable stewpack (from frozen state) and stir round until thawed.

4 Sprinkle Bisto over meat and vegetables then blend in water. Season to taste and bring to the boil.

5 Lower heat. Cover. Simmer 1¾ to 2 hours or until meat is tender. Remove from heat and divide equally into four separate lots.

Chili Beef (serves 4 to 6)

Add the following to Lot 1:

½ to 1 level tsp chili powder (it is a fiery spice so take care!), 4 level tbsp tomato purée and 1 can (about 15¼oz or 432g) American red kidney beans, first well-drained. Heat through until bubbling.

Serve with rice and a green salad.

Exotic Beef (serves 4 to 6)
Add the following to Lot 2:

1 to 1½oz (25 to 40g) canned Madagascan green peppers (the kind used for pepper steaks), 1 crushed garlic clove and 2 tbsp brandy. Heat through until bubbling.

Serve with thick slices of crusty French bread and a large mixed salad.

Beef Madras (serves 4 to 6)
Add the following to Lot 3:

3 rounded tsp mild curry paste, 1 heaped tsp garam masala, ¼ level tsp garlic granules (or a clove of garlic, crushed), 1 rounded tbsp desiccated coconut, 2 rounded tsp mango chutney, 2 rounded tsp tomato purée and 1 level tsp salt. Heat through until bubbling.

Serve with Basmati rice and side dishes (sambals) of coconut, sliced tomato and onions, chutney and coarsely chopped peanuts.

Paprika Cream Beef (serves 4 to 6)
Add the following to Lot 4:

1 rounded tbsp paprika, 2 heaped tbsp tomato purée, ½ to 1 level tsp caraway seeds and 1 crushed garlic clove. Heat through until bubbling. Transfer to warm serving dish and stir in 1 carton (5oz or 142ml) soured cream. Accompany with small pasta.

Fruited Aitchbone Braise (serves 6 to 8)

4lb (2 kg) boned aitchbone, rolled and tied at 1 inch (2¼cm) intervals
1 level tbsp flour mixed with 4 heaped tsp Onion Bisto
1oz (25g) margarine
½pt (275ml) water
2 large celery stalks, thinly sliced
3 medium trimmed and slit leeks, well-washed and sliced
1 level tsp salt
pepper to taste
1 rounded tbsp tomato purée
¼ level tsp thyme
1 can (15oz or 425g) apricot halves including syrup
4 medium tomatoes, skinned, de-seeded and chopped
1 level tsp Dijon mustard

1 Coat joint all over with flour-and-Bisto mixture.
2 Heat margarine in large and heavy-based saucepan. Add aitchbone. Fry until golden brown all over. Remove to plate.
3 Pour water into pan then add all remaining ingredients. Stir until boiling.
4 Replace meat. Lower heat. Cover. Simmer gently for about 2½ hours or until meat is tender.

5 Remove to board, cut into thick slices and arrange on warm dish. Coat with sauce which should be purée-like in appearance.

Serve with boiled potatoes and green vegetables.

One-pot Beef Dinner (serves 6)

8oz (225g) button onions or shallots
12oz (350g) carrots, cut into 2 inch (5cm) lengths
2 large celery stalks, cut into 2 inch (5cm) lengths
2oz (50g) butter or margarine
3lb (1½kg) piece of rolled brisket
6 rounded tsp Bisto
1½pt (just under 1 litre) water
2 large leeks, slit, well-washed and cut into 2 inch (5cm) lengths

1 Fry the prepared vegetables, except leeks, in the butter or margarine in a large pan or flameproof casserole for 5 minutes. Move to one side. Add meat. Fry until browned on all sides.
2 Blend the Bisto to a smooth paste with a little of the water. Blend in remaining water. Pour over the meat and vegetables.
3 Cover the pan and simmer gently for 1¾ hours. Add the leeks and simmer for a further ½ hour. Serve with jacket potatoes.

Tip
When trimming leeks, leave on 3 inches (7½cm) of the green part.

Beef Cobbler (serves 4)

2oz (50g) butter or margarine
1 large onion, chopped
4 medium celery stalks, thinly sliced
1oz (25g) flour
2 level tsp Bisto
salt and pepper
1lb (500g) chuck steak, cut into 1 inch (2½cm) cubes
1 can (14oz or 400g) tomatoes
1 small bay leaf
2 level tsp caster sugar

Cobbler topping
8oz (225g) self-raising flour
1 level tsp salt
1 level tsp mixed herbs
2oz (50g) butter or margarine
7 tbsp cold milk to mix
beaten egg for brushing

1 Melt butter or margarine in pan. Add onion and celery. Fry gently, covered, until soft. Transfer to shallow ovenproof dish.

2 Mix together flour and Bisto. Season to taste with salt and pepper. Add steak cubes. Toss over and over until well-coated.

3 Add to remaining fat in frying pan. Fry fairly briskly, turning, until pieces of meat are evenly browned. Tip into dish over fried vegetables.

4 Coat with tomatoes. Add bay leaf. Sprinkle with sugar. Cover. Cook 2 hours in oven set to 350°F (180°C), Gas 4.

5 After 1½ hours, make cobbler topping: sift flour and salt into bowl. Toss in herbs. Rub in butter or margarine.

6 Sprinkle milk over dry ingredients in one go. Mix to a dough with round-topped knife.

7 Turn out onto lightly-floured board. Knead quickly till smooth. Roll out to ½ inch (1¼cm) in thickness. Cut into 10 to 12 rounds with 2 inch (5cm) plain cutter.

8 Uncover casserole. Arrange cobbler rounds in an overlapping border on top of filling. Brush with beaten egg.

9 Return to oven for a further 30 minutes.

Spoon on to plates and accompany with potatoes and green vegetables to taste.

West Country Creamy Beef Stew (serves 4 to 6)

1½lb (750g) chuck steak, cubed
1oz (25g) flour
6 rounded tsp Bisto
1 tbsp salad oil
1oz (25g) butter or margarine
8oz (225g) small onions or shallots
¾pt (425ml) dry cider
¼pt (150ml) water
8oz (225g) dessert apples, peeled, cored and diced
1 carton (5oz or 142ml) soured cream
salt and pepper to taste

1 Toss cubed meat in flour and Bisto.

2 Heat oil and butter or margarine in a large pan, add onion and fry for 3 minutes.

3 Add coated meat and fry quickly to brown evenly.

4 Put into casserole and cover with cider and water.

5 Cover and cook for 1½ hours at 350°F (180°C), Gas 4.

6 Remove casserole from oven and add diced apples. Cover and cook for a further 30 minutes.

7 Stir in soured cream and adjust seasoning to taste. Serve with boiled rice.

West Country beef stew

Old-fashioned steak and kidney casserole

Beef Stew and Caraway Dumplings (serves 4)

8oz (225g) small onions or shallots
3 tbsp salad oil
1½lb (750g) shin of beef, cut into small cubes
1 rounded tsp flour
4 rounded tsp Bisto
1pt (575ml) water
1 small swede, cubed
salt and pepper to taste

Dumplings
4oz (100 to 125g) self-raising flour
pinch of salt
2oz (50g) shredded suet
1 level tsp caraway seeds
cold water

1 Fry the onions in the oil till glazed and lightly golden brown. Remove from the pan.
2 Dust the beef in flour and fry in the fat until brown on all sides. Add the onions to the meat.
3 Blend the Bisto to a smooth paste with a little of the water and then add the remaining water.
4 Pour the Bisto liquid over the meat. Add the swede. Season.
5 Cover the pan and simmer slowly for 1½ hours.
6 Meanwhile make the dumplings: sieve the flour and salt, add the suet and caraway seeds, mix to a soft dough with water, and divide into 4 balls.
7 Add the dumplings to the stew and cook for a further 15-20 minutes.

Beef Crumble (serves 6)

1 large onion, grated
1lb (500g) raw lean minced beef
1 tbsp salad oil
4 rounded tsp Bisto
¾pt (425ml) water
salt and pepper to taste
1 packet sage-and-onion stuffing mix
2oz (50g) flour
3oz (75g) butter
3oz (75g) Cheddar cheese, grated

1 Fry the onion and mince in oil until lightly browned, fork-stirring all the time.
2 Blend the Bisto to a smooth paste with a little water. Add the remaining water.
3 Add the Bisto liquid and seasoning to the meat, and stir over medium heat until lightly thickened.
4 Put the stuffing mix and flour into a bowl. Add the butter, cut into tiny cubes, and 2oz (50g) of the cheese. Mix together.
5 Put the mince mixture into a greased ovenproof dish and sprinkle the stuffing crumble mixture over the top. Sprinkle with the remaining grated cheese.

6 Bake for 40-45 minutes at 350°F (180°C), Gas 4. Serve with green vegetables.

Irish-style Beef Casserole (serves 4 to 6)

1½lb (750g) chuck steak, cut into 1 inch (2½cm) cubes
1½oz (40g) butter
1 tsp salad oil
1oz (25g) flour
3 heaped tsp Bisto
½pt (275ml) water
1 tsp Worcestershire sauce
1 tbsp tomato purée
salt and pepper to taste
4oz (100 to 125g) onion, sliced
2 medium carrots, sliced
1 large celery stalk, sliced
6 medium peeled potatoes, halved and parboiled
8 streaky bacon rashers, rolled

1 Make sure beef is very dry; after washing it, wipe it with paper towels.
2 Heat butter and oil in large pan. Add beef cubes, a few at a time. Fry until crisp and brown all over. Remove to plate.
3 Stir flour and Bisto into remaining butter and oil in pan. Cook 2 to 3 minutes to form a roux. Gradually blend in water.
4 Cook, stirring, until sauce comes to boil and thickens. Add Worcestershire sauce and tomato purée, then season to taste.
5 Place onion, carrots and celery over base of greased casserole. Arrange meat on top, then coat with the sauce. Cover. Cook 1¾ hours in oven set to 350°C (180°C), Gas 4.
6 Uncover. Add potatoes. Re-cover. Cook a further ½ to ¾ hour.

Just before serving, grill bacon rolls and use to garnish the casserole.

Casseroled Beef Olives (serves 4)

Stuffing
3oz (75g) fresh white breadcrumbs
3oz (75g) ham or bacon, chopped
1 heaped tbsp chopped parsley
½ level tsp mixed herbs
finely grated peel of ½ lemon
salt and pepper to taste
1½oz (40g) margarine, melted
beaten egg to bind

To complete beef olives
1lb (500g) flank or topside, cut into 4 slices
1oz (25g) flour seasoned with salt and pepper
2 medium onions, sliced
3 tbsp salad oil
1 bay leaf
4 rounded tsp Bisto
1pt (575ml) water

1 Combine stuffing ingredients.
2 Batten out the meat and spread with the stuffing. Roll up into parcels and tie together with thin string. Toss in seasoned flour.
3 Brown meat and onion in oil for 5 minutes. Transfer to casserole. Add bay leaf.
4 Mix Bisto to a smooth paste with a little of the water. Blend in remaining water and pour into casserole.
5 Cover and cook for 2 hours at 350°F (180°C), Gas 4.
6 Remove string before serving.
  Accompany with creamed potatoes and green vegetables.

Beef and Cabbage Casserole (serves 4)

1lb (500g) beef shin, cut into 1 inch (2½cm) cubes
3 heaped tsp Onion Bisto
2 tbsp salad oil
½pt (275ml) water
salt and pepper to taste
½ small white cabbage, shredded
1 can (15oz or 425g) ready-to-serve tomato soup

1 Coat cubes of beef all over with Bisto. Heat oil in pan. Add beef. Fry until well-browned, turning.
2 Stir in any left-over Onion Bisto. Gradually blend in water. Season to taste. Bring to boil.
3 Place half the cabbage into ovenproof casserole. Top with meat and gravy mixture. Cover with rest of cabbage.

4 Coat with soup. Cover. Cook 2 hours in cool oven set to 325°F (160°C), Gas 3.
  Serve with boiled potatoes.

Corned Beef Fritters (serves 4)

Make batter exactly as given in recipe for Italian fritto misto on page 113. Chill 1 can (12oz or 340g) corned beef in the refrigerator. Open can. Cut meat into 8 slices. Coat with batter. Fry in deep hot oil until crisp and golden. Drain on paper towels.
  Serve with pickles and chips.

Beef and Potato Shred Pie (serves 4)

1lb (500g) raw minced beef, as lean as possible
1 large garlic clove, crushed
2 level tbsp tomato purée
½pt (275ml) water
1 cube of sugar
½ level tsp salt
1 tbsp brown ketchup
3 rounded tsp Onion Bisto
2 extra tbsp cold water
1 level tsp mixed herbs
1lb (500g) cold cooked potatoes
1oz (25g) butter, melted
1 level tbsp lightly toasted breadcrumbs

1 Place first 7 ingredients into sturdy pan. Bring to boil. Skim. Lower heat. Cover. Simmer ¾ hour, stirring from time to time to prevent mince from becoming lumpy.
2 To thicken, mix Bisto smoothly with 2 tbsp water. Add to mince with herbs. Bring up to boil. Tip into heatproof pie-dish.
3 Grate potatoes directly over meat, trying to form as even a layer as possible.
4 Trickle butter over the top, then sprinkle with crumbs. Heat through and brown potato topping under a hot grill.
  Serve with green vegetables.

Beef and potato shred pie

Beef and Cheesy Potato Shred Pie (serves 4)

Make exactly as above but substitute 1½oz (40g) grated Cheddar cheese for the crumbs.

Curried Beef and Potato Shred Pie (serves 4)

Make exactly as beef and potato shred pie, but add 1 level tbsp seedless raisins and 2 level tsp curry powder at the same time as the ketchup. Grate potatoes over top as described, trickle with butter, then sprinkle with 1 level tbsp desiccated coconut. Brown under a hot grill.

Serve with chutney and salad.

Shepherd's Pie (serves 4 to 5)

1oz (25g) butter, margarine or dripping
1lb (500g) raw minced beef
3 level tsp cornflour
3 rounded tsp Onion Bisto
¾pt (425ml) water
salt and pepper to taste

Topping
1½lb (750g) freshly boiled potatoes
1oz (25g) butter or margarine
warm milk
salt and pepper to taste

1 Heat fat in pan. Add meat. Fry briskly, fork-stirring continuously, until it is golden-brown and crumbly.
2 Stir in cornflour and Bisto. Gradually blend in water. Season. Cook, stirring, until mixture comes to boil and thickens.
3 Cover. Simmer gently for ¾ hour. Stir from time to time to prevent sticking.
4 Tip meat into deepish casserole and leave to cool off slightly. Meanwhile, mash potatoes with butter then beat until smooth with the milk. Season.
5 Pile over meat, then brown about 20 minutes in oven set to 375°F (190°C), Gas 5.
Serve with green vegetables.

Cheesy Shepherd's Pie (serves 4 to 5)

Sprinkle potatoes with 2oz (50g) grated Cheddar cheese before browning in the oven.

Minced Beef Pie (serves 6)

shortcrust pastry made with 6oz (175g) flour and 3oz (75g) fat (or use 9oz (250g) pastry mix)
1lb (500g) raw lean minced beef
2 level tsp Bisto
5 tbsp canned evaporated milk (unsweetened)
4 level tbsp tomato ketchup
1oz (25g) fresh white breadcrumbs
2oz (50g) onion, grated
½ level tsp mixed herbs
salt and pepper to taste
4 skinned tomatoes, chopped
1 medium green pepper, de-seeded and chopped
2oz (50g) mushrooms, trimmed and sliced with stalks
1oz (25g) butter or margarine

1 Roll out pastry fairly thinly and use to line an 8 inch (20cm) deepish heatproof pie-plate with rim. (The 'old-fashioned' enamel plates are excellent.) To facilitate removal, lightly grease the plate first. Ridge pastry edge with fork.
2 For filling, mix beef thoroughly with next six ingredients. Season to taste. Spoon into pastry case. Smooth evenly with wet knife.
3 Bake ¾ hour in oven set to 375°F (190°C), Gas 5, when pastry should be golden and meat filling firm. If not, cook an extra ¼ hour.
4 To make topping, fry tomatoes, green pepper and mushrooms in the butter or margarine for ¼ hour. Keep heat low and pan covered. Uncover. Boil briskly until minimal liquid remains. Spoon over pie. Cut into wedges.
Serve hot with jacket potatoes and salad.

Savoury Mince and Vegetables (serves 4)

1lb (500g) raw lean minced beef
1 large onion, coarsely grated
2 medium carrots, coarsely grated
1 medium celery stalk, sliced
½ level tsp mixed herbs
3 rounded tsp Bisto
½pt (250ml) water

1 Put meat, vegetables and herbs into saucepan. Add Bisto blended smoothly with water.
2 Bring to boil, stirring. Lower heat and cover. Simmer 1 hour.
3 Serve with creamed or boiled potatoes and brussels sprouts or cauliflower.

One-pot beef dinner

Beef cobbler

Minced Beef Loaf (serves 4 to 6)

Useful for those occasions when remains of the weekend joint are there to use up.

4oz (125g) streaky bacon, rinds removed
12oz (350g) cooked beef
1 medium onion, cut into eighths
2oz (50g) fresh white breadcrumbs
1 level tbsp chopped parsley
1 × Grade 3 (standard) egg
½ can condensed mushroom soup
salt and pepper to taste
2 level tsp Bisto

Garnish
slices of tomato and cucumber
sprigs of watercress

1 Mince bacon, beef and onion. Add all remaining ingredients. Mix thoroughly.
2 Line 1lb (500g) oblong loaf tin with foil. Brush with melted fat. Fill with beef mixture. Smooth top with knife.
3 Cover with foil. Cook 1 hour in centre of oven set to 350°F (180°C), Gas 4.
4 Turn out immediately if to be served hot. If not, leave till cold in the tin.
5 Turn out and garnish with tomato, cucumber and watercress as shown in the picture.
   If serving hot, accompany with Bisto gravy, potatoes and green vegetables. If serving cold, accompany with potato salad and pickles.

Jiffy Burgers (serves 4)

1lb (500g) lean raw minced beef
3 heaped tsp Onion Bisto
1 tbsp water

1 Mix all ingredients well together with fork.
2 With damp hands, shape into 8 burgers.
3 Grill or fry about 7 to 8 minutes, turning once.
   Serve, with tomato ketchup or mustard, in split and toasted hamburger buns. Alternatively, serve with mashed potatoes and vegetables.

Souffléd Shepherd's Casserole (serves 4)

2 medium onions, sliced
1oz (25g) butter or margarine
2 tbsp salad oil
12oz (350g) raw lean minced beef
4 rounded tsp Bisto
¾pt (425ml) water
2 tbsp tomato purée
12oz (350g) freshly boiled mashed potatoes
2 × Grade 3 (standard) eggs, separated
2oz (50g) Cheddar cheese, grated

1 Fry the onion in the butter or margarine and oil for 3 minutes.
2 Add the minced beef and cook until lightly browned.
3 Mix Bisto to a paste with a little water.
4 Stir in the remaining water and tomato purée.
5 Add to the beef and simmer for 10 minutes, stirring.
6 Put into a greased oven-proof dish.
7 Beat the potato with the egg yolks and half the cheese.
8 Fold in the egg whites, stiffly beaten.
9 Fork over the meat mixture and sprinkle with the remaining grated cheese. Bake 15 to 20 minutes in oven set to 375°F (190°C), Gas 5.
   Serve with green vegetables to taste.

Luxury Beef Stroganoff (serves 8)

2lb (1kg) rump steak, fat trimmed
3oz (75g) butter
2 tsp salad oil
2 rounded tsp Onion Bisto
2 rounded tbsp tomato purée
4 rounded tbsp grated pickled cucumber
2 cartons (*each* 5oz or 142ml) soured cream
salt and pepper to taste
2 heaped tbsp chopped parsley

1 Cut rump steak into thin strips. Heat butter and oil in large frying pan.
2 Add steak. Fry over high heat for about 7 minutes, turning frequently.
3 Stir in Onion Bisto, tomato purée and pickled cucumber. Heat through a further 5 minutes.
4 Stir in soured cream and season to taste with salt and pepper.
   Transfer to a serving dish and sprinkle with parsley. Accompany with freshly boiled rice.

Pennywise Beef Stroganoff (serves 4)

1oz (25g) flour
2 level tsp Bisto
1lb (500g) chuck steak, cut into 1 inch (2½cm) strips
2oz (50g) butter or margarine
2 medium onions, peeled and sliced
4oz (125g) trimmed mushrooms, sliced
½pt (275ml) water
4 level tbsp tomato ketchup
1 carton (5oz or 142ml) natural yogurt
chopped parsley
triangles of toast for garnish.

1 Mix flour and Bisto together in a small basin. Add strips of meat and toss thoroughly to coat.

2 Heat butter or margarine in medium-sized saucepan with a heavy base. Add meat and fry until evenly browned.

3 Add onions and mushrooms. Fry until soft, stirring from time to time. Blend in water and ketchup. Bring slowly to the boil. Lower heat. Cover.

4 Simmer 1½ to 1¾ hours, when meat should be tender and gravy richly coloured.

5 Turn into a serving dish, stir in yogurt. Sprinkle top with parsley, then surround with triangles of toast.

Steak Tartare (serves 1)

So many people are puzzled over Steak Tartare and have asked me repeatedly if it really *is* made with raw beef that I believe a recipe and short explanation are needed. Yes, raw meat is *always* used and although the dish is an acquired taste, it is very much appreciated by gourmets and slimmers. The essential thing is to use top-quality rump or fillet steak, remove every grain of fat and gristle, and mince it *finely* at home.

For 1 serving allow 6oz (175g) minced meat. Stand on the centre of a large dinner plate and hollow out the centre with the back of a spoon. Sprinkle with chopped parsley and drop in an egg yolk. Serve with tiny side dishes of

1 small chopped onion
2 chopped anchovy fillets
1 level tsp chopped capers

The technique is to help oneself to the side dishes and mix them into the beef, egg yolk and parsley. The best accompaniments are rye bread or pumpernickel.

Note

Steak Tartare does come from Russia and is named after Tartar fighters who went into battle with steaks as well as weapons!

Meaty Minestrone (serves 6)

2oz (50g) haricot beans, soaked overnight, then parboiled in unsalted water till almost tender
1 medium onion, chopped
2 medium carrots, cut into small cubes
3 medium celery stalks, thinly sliced
½ small green cabbage, shredded
1 large leek, well-washed and thinly sliced
1 large garlic clove, crushed
1 can (14oz or 400g) tomatoes
1 large raw potato, cubed
4oz (100 to 125g) lean minced beef, raw
4 rounded tsp Bisto
1½pt (just under 1 litre) water
2oz (50g) long grain rice
salt and pepper to taste
3 heaped tbsp chopped parsley
grated Parmesan cheese

1 Drain beans and put into a pan with the onion, carrot, celery, cabbage, leek, garlic, tomatoes, potato and minced beef.

2 Mix Bisto to a smooth paste with a little water. Blend in remaining water and add to the pan.

3 Simmer for 45 minutes.

4 Add the rice and simmer for a further 20 minutes. Adjust seasoning if necessary.

Stir in the chopped parsley and serve immediately, sprinkled with the grated Parmesan cheese.

Steak tartare

Luxury Bolognese Sauce (serves 6)

1 tbsp salad oil
4oz (125g) onion, grated
1 to 2 large garlic cloves, crushed
3oz (75g) unsmoked gammon, finely chopped
1lb (500g) raw minced beef
4 heaped tsp Bisto
1 can (16oz or 450g) tomatoes
2 rounded tbsp tomato purée
2 tsp granulated sugar
½pt (275ml) dry red wine
1 level tsp basil or oregano
1 bay leaf
4 heaped tbsp soured cream
salt and pepper to taste

1 Heat oil in heavy pan. Add onion, garlic and gammon. Fry gently until pale gold.
2 Stir in meat. Fry a little more briskly until dark brown and crumbly, breaking it up with a fork all the time.
3 Mix in Bisto, tomatoes, tomato purée, sugar, wine, basil, bay leaf, cream and seasoning. Bring to boil, stirring. Lower heat. Cover. Simmer very slowly for 2 hours. Stir occasionally. Add cream and correct the seasoning.

    Serve over freshly cooked spaghetti and pass grated Parmesan cheese separately.

Economical Bolognese Sauce (serves 6)

Omit bacon. Use beef stock (cube and water) instead of wine. Do not add cream.

Italian-style Lasagne (serves 8)

8oz (225g) leaves of lasagne
boiling salted water
2 tsp salad oil
luxury or economical Bolognese sauce
1pt (575ml) well-flavoured and freshly made cheese sauce
1oz (25g) grated Parmesan cheese
1oz (25g) butter

1 Cook lasagne leaves, a few at a time, in boiling salted water—with oil added—for about 10 to 12 minutes.
2 Drain. Rinse carefully under cold water. Stand on a clean tea towel to drain.
3 To assemble the lasagne, fill an oblong heatproof dish (well-buttered and not too deep) with alternate layers of lasagne, Bolognese sauce and cheese sauce.
4 Finish with a top layer of cheese sauce. Sprinkle with cheese. Dot with flakes of butter. Reheat ½ hour in oven set to 400°F (200°C), Gas 6.

    Serve with salad.

Lasagne Verdi (serves 8)

Make as above but use green lasagne.

Steak Pizzaiola

Minced beef loaf

Steak Pizzaiola (serves 4)

1½lb (750g) skinned tomatoes, chopped
2 tbsp salad oil
3 level tsp Onion Bisto
1 large garlic clove, crushed
2 level tbsp finely chopped parsley
½ level tsp basil
½ level tsp marjoram
2 tsp lemon juice
1 rounded tsp caster sugar
salt and pepper to taste
4 rump or sirloin steaks, each about 1 inch (2½cm)
  thick and weighing 4 to 6oz (100 to 175g)

1 Put all ingredients, except steaks, into pan. Bring
slowly to boil, stirring.
2 Lower heat. Bubble gently for about 20 minutes or
until sauce has thickened. Stir from time to time to
prevent sauce from catching over base of pan.
3 Grill steaks according to preference (well done,
medium or rare).
4 Transfer to warm dinner plates and coat with equal
amounts of sauce.
  Accompany with freshly cooked spaghetti.

Italian Beef in Wine (serves 8)

A full-flavoured beef stew that is classic Italian and a marvellous party dish.

3lb (1½kg) chuck steak
2 tbsp salad oil
8oz (225g) onions, chopped
4 large garlic cloves, crushed
8oz (225g) mixed root vegetables, diced
4 heaped tsp Bisto
1 can (16oz or 450g) tomatoes
4oz (125g) Parma ham, chopped (or, for economy, use lean bacon)
¾pt (425ml) Barolo red wine
bouquet garni
salt and pepper to taste

1 Cube meat, removing all traces of fat. Heat oil in large pan. Add meat, a few pieces at a time. Fry until well-sealed and brown. Remove to plate temporarily.
2 Add onions, garlic and root vegetables to rest of oil in pan. Fry till pale gold. Stir in Bisto, tomatoes, ham or bacon, wine and bouquet garni. Season.
3 Replace meat. Bring to boil, stirring. Skim. Lower heat. Cover. Simmer over *minimal heat* for 3 to 4 hours, when meat should be very tender. Stir occasionally.
   Serve with polenta (page 85) and green vegetables to taste.

Stuffed Peppers Bolognese (serves 6)

6 medium green peppers
1 large onion, chopped
3 rashers back bacon, chopped
2 tbsp salad oil
8oz (225g) raw lean minced beef
3 rounded tbsp tomato purée
1 large garlic clove, crushed
4oz (100 to 125g) trimmed mushrooms, chopped
2 medium carrots, grated
4 rounded tsp Bisto
¾pt (425ml) water
4oz (100 to 125g) cooked rice
salt and pepper to taste

1 Cut a thin slice from the stalk end of each pepper. Remove the seeds. Put peppers into a pan of boiling water and simmer for 5 minutes.
2 Fry the onion and chopped bacon in oil for 5 minutes.
3 Add the minced beef and cook until lightly browned, fork-stirring all the time.
4 Stir in the tomato purée, garlic, mushrooms and carrot. This is the Bolognese sauce.
5 Blend Bisto to a paste with a little of the cold water. Blend in remaining water and stir into Bolognese sauce.

6 Bring to the boil and simmer for 5 minutes.
7 Bind the rice with some of the Bolognese sauce. Season.
8 Sit peppers upright in a casserole and fill with the rice mixture.
9 Spoon the remaining sauce around the peppers.
10 Cover the casserole and cook for 1 hour at 350°F (180°C), Gas 4.

Sauerbraten (serves 6)

A favourite and oldtime German dish which should be prepared 3 days in advance. It is excellent with boiled potatoes and cooked red cabbage.

3lb (1½kg) piece of rolled blade bone or thick rump of beef
½pt (275ml) water
½pt (275ml) malt vinegar
1 level tsp coarsely ground pepper
1 large onion, sliced
2 large carrots, sliced
1 bay leaf
2oz (50g) butter or margarine, melted
5 rounded tsp Bisto
½pt (275ml) red wine
1½oz (40g) caster sugar

1 Put the beef into a deep container with a lid.
2 Heat the water, vinegar, pepper, onion, carrots and bay leaf for 10 minutes. Allow to cool.
3 Pour the spiced vinegar over the meat and cover the container. Keep in a cool place for 3 days, turning daily.
4 Drain the meat, reserving the liquid. Brown on all sides in the melted butter or margarine.
5 Strain the spiced vinegar and add the carrot and onion to the meat.
6 Mix the Bisto to a smooth paste with a little of the wine. Add the remaining wine and ½ pint (275ml) of the spiced vinegar with sugar. Pour over the meat.
7 Bring to the boil, and cover the pan. Simmer very gently for 2½ hours.
   Serve sliced, with pan juices.

Boeuf Bourguignonne (serves 4 to 6)

2oz (50g) butter or margarine
1 tbsp salad oil
8oz (225g) onions, chopped
8oz (225g) unsmoked gammon, coarsely chopped
2lb (1kg) blade bone or skirt steak, cut into cubes or squares
1 level tbsp cornflour
3 heaped tsp Bisto
½pt (275ml) dry red wine
bouquet garni
12 shallots or small onions
2 large garlic cloves, crushed
8oz (225g) button mushrooms, trimmed but left whole
salt and pepper to taste

1 Heat butter or margarine and oil in large pan. Add onions and bacon. Fry gently ¼ hour.
2 Move to edges of pan. Add beef cubes. Fry a little more briskly until well sealed and brown, stirring.
3 Stir in cornflour and Bisto. Gradually blend in wine. Add bouquet garni, shallots or small onions, and the crushed garlic.
4 Bring to boil, stirring. Lower heat. Cover. Simmer 1¾ to 2¼ hours or till meat is tender. Add mushrooms.
5 Cook a further 5 minutes. Season to taste.

Serve with freshly boiled potatoes and a large green salad.

Boeuf á la Mode (serves 6 to 8)

A French pot-roast which is laced with red wine and brandy.

3lb (1½kg) chuck steak in one piece
1 large garlic clove, halved
salt and pepper
2 level tbsp flour mixed with 3 heaped tsp Bisto
2oz (50g) butter
1 tbsp salad oil
¾pt (425ml) dry red wine
12 shallots or small onions
8oz (225g) carrots, thickly sliced
bouquet garni
1 pig's trotter, chopped into medium-sized pieces
1 level tsp salt
8oz (225g) trimmed mushrooms, sliced with stalks
4 tbsp brandy

1 Wash and dry steak. Rub all over with cut garlic clove. Sprinkle with salt and pepper.
2 Coat thickly with flour and Bisto mixture. Heat butter and oil in sturdy pan. Add meat. Fry all over till golden-brown, keeping heat fairly brisk.

3 Pour wine into pan then add all remaining ingredients except mushrooms and brandy. Bring slowly to boil. Lower heat and cover.
4 Simmer gently 2½ to 3 hours or until meat is tender. Add mushrooms and brandy. Cook ¼ hour. Remove meat to board and carve into medium-thick slices.
5 Arrange on warm platter. Surround with vegetables and coat with sauce from pan.

Serve with boiled potatoes and green vegetables to taste.

Boeuf en Daube (serves 6)

A classic French stew with a heart-warming flavour.

3lb (1½kg) chuck or blade bone steak
4oz (100 to 125g) gammon
4oz (100 to 125g) carrots
8oz (225g) onions
8oz (225g) tomatoes, skinned
2 garlic cloves
2 tbsp salad oil
2 rounded tsp Bisto
bouquet garni
¼pt (150ml) dry red wine
salt and pepper to taste

1 Cut meat into fairly small cubes. Chop gammon coarsely. Thinly slice carrots and onions. Chop tomatoes and garlic.
2 Heat oil in heavy-based pan. Add gammon and prepared vegetables. Fry gently until pale gold, allowing about ¼ hour.
3 Move to edge of pan. Add beef cubes. Fry fairly briskly for about 5 minutes, turning frequently. Stir in Bisto.
4 Add bouquet garni and wine. Mix well. Transfer to casserole. Season to taste. Cover. Cook 2 to 2½ hours in oven set to 325°F (160°C), Gas 3.

Serve with green vegetables and boiled potatoes.

Chinese-style Beef (serves 4 to 6)

1lb (500g) beef shin, cut into thin strips
1 level tsp salt
2 rounded tsp granulated sugar
1 tbsp soy sauce
3 tbsp salad oil
1oz (25g) flour
3 rounded tsp Onion Bisto
¾pt (425ml) water
1 can (11oz or 300g) bean sprouts, drained
3oz (75g) button mushrooms, sliced
crispy fried noodles for serving

1 Put meat into shallow glass or enamel bowl. Add salt, sugar and soy sauce. Toss over and over with spoon. Cover. Refrigerate 1 hour.
2 Heat oil in pan. Drain meat and add. Sprinkle with flour. Cook 1 minute, turning.
3 Mix Onion Bisto to smooth paste with some of the water. Pour in rest of water. Add to pan of meat with soy sauce mixture in which meat was standing.
4 Bring gently to boil, stirring. Lower heat. Cover. Simmer 1 hour or until meat is tender, stirring occasionally. Add bean sprouts and mushrooms and cook a further 5 minutes.
5 Transfer to a serving dish and add a border of crispy fried noodles.
  Accompany with rice.

Crispy fried noodles
These are available in packet form, ready to fry. Alternatively, make your own by cooking egg noodles in boiling salted water until tender, then draining and deep-frying.

Beef á la Lindstrom (serves 4)

My favourite beefburgers from Sweden. Where the name comes from, or why beetroot is added, I've never discovered, but they are exceptionally tasty, piquant and easy to make.

1lb (500g) raw minced beef
8oz (225g) freshly boiled potatoes, finely mashed
3 rounded tsp Onion Bisto
4oz (100 to 125g) pickled beetroot, grated
1 level tbsp drained capers, chopped
4 tbsp undiluted evaporated milk
white pepper to taste
dripping or margarine for frying

1 Combine beef with potatoes, Bisto, beetroot, capers, milk and pepper to taste.
2 Shape into 8 cakes. Fry or grill in hot dripping or margarine for about 8 to 10 minutes or until cooked through and brown, turning twice.
  Serve with potatoes tossed in butter and a mixture of green vegetables. Cranberry sauce makes an excellent accompaniment.

Chinese-style beef

New England Glazed Brisket (serves 8)

An unusual recipe for salted brisket which I tasted in the kitchens of a Boston cook. She was also responsible for the two very special sauces to go with the beef.

4lb (2kg) salted beef brisket, boned but unrolled and left flat
cold water
1 small onion, sliced
1 large garlic clove, crushed
12 peppercorns
1 bay leaf

Glaze
4oz (125g) soft brown sugar
2oz (50g) fresh white breadcrumbs
2 level tsp Onion Bisto
2 tbsp clear honey

1 Put brisket into large pan that is shallow rather than deep. Cover with cold water. Bring to boil. Drain.
2 Pour in sufficient fresh cold water to cover beef by about 1 inch (2½cm). Add onion, garlic, peppercorns and bay leaf.
3 Simmer gently for about 3 hours or until meat is tender. Lift out of pan and drain. Trim off excess fat.
4 Stand, fat side uppermost, in baking tin. For glaze, mix all ingredients well together. Spread over fat.
5 Cook about 20 to 25 minutes—or until glaze melts— in oven set to 350°F (180°C), Gas 4.

Serve with the two sauces which follow, coleslaw and very fresh brown bread.

Mustard cream sauce
1½ level tbsp powdered mustard
1 level tsp flour
¼pt (150ml) + 4 tbsp single cream
1 egg yolk
1 level tsp caster sugar
4 tbsp mild vinegar
salt and white pepper to taste

1 Combine mustard and flour smoothly with 3 tbsp cream.
2 Heat rest of cream to lukewarm. Whisk in mustard mixture. Take out 2 tbsp and mix with yolk. Return to pan.
3 Add sugar and cook, whisking constantly, until thickened and smooth.
4 Stir in vinegar. Season to taste with salt and pepper.

Horseradish and sour cream sauce
2 cartons (*each* 5oz or 142ml) soured cream
2 level tbsp prepared horseradish
1 level tbsp prepared American mustard
1 level tbsp finely chopped onion
1 level tbsp finely chopped fresh dill (optional)

1 Mix all ingredients thoroughly.
2 Cover and refrigerate until ready to serve.

Carbonnade of Beef (serves 4)

2oz (50g) butter or margarine
2 medium onions, peeled and chopped
2 garlic cloves, chopped
2 level tsp Bisto
1oz (25g) flour
salt and pepper
1lb (500g) blade bone steak, cut into 1 inch (2½cm) cubes
1 tsp malt vinegar
1 level tsp Demerara sugar
1 tsp Worcestershire sauce
½pt (275ml) stout
4 × 1 inch (2½cm) thick slices of French bread
French mustard

Garnish
chopped parsley

1 Heat butter or margarine in pan. Add onions and garlic. Fry gently until pale gold. Transfer to a fairly shallow ovenproof casserole.
2 Combine Bisto with flour and salt and pepper to taste. Add beef cubes. Toss well to mix. Tip into remaining fat in pan. Fry briskly until well sealed and brown.
3 Transfer meat to casserole. Pour vinegar, sugar, Worcestershire sauce and stout into pan in which vegetables and meat were fried. Bring to boil, stirring.
4 Pour into casserole dish. Cover with lid or foil. Cook 2 hours in oven set to 325°F (160°C), Gas 3. Uncover. Top with slices of French bread, spread thickly with mustard.
5 Return to oven. Cook, uncovered, a further 20 to 30 minutes or till bread is crisp and golden. Spoon onto plates, sprinkle with parsley.

Serve with boiled potatoes and a green salad.

Tip
This is a Belgian classic dish, often thickened with about 1½oz (40g) brown breadcrumbs instead of the flour.

Castilian Hash (serves 4 to 6)

1 large onion, chopped
2 tbsp salad oil
1lb (500g) raw lean minced beef
1 rounded tbsp tomato purée
1 can (14oz or 400g) tomatoes
3 rounded tsp Bisto
½pt (275ml) water
2oz (50g) Spanish stuffed olives, halved
2 rounded tbsp seedless raisins
6oz (175g) chick peas, soaked overnight and drained

Pennywise beef stroganoff

1 Fry the onion in the oil for 3 minutes.
2 Add the minced beef and cook until light brown and crumbly, fork-stirring all the time. Stir in the tomato purée and the canned tomatoes.
3 Blend Bisto to smooth paste with a little of the water. Stir in remainder.
4 Pour into pan over meat mixture and stir in well.
5 Add all remaining ingredients. Bring to boil. Lower heat. Cover pan.
6 Simmer gently for 1 to 1¼ hours or until chick peas are tender.
   Serve with mashed potatoes and a mixed salad.

Short-cut Chili (serves 6)

For those who want a simpler version of traditional chili, this recipe should suit admirably.

1lb (500g) lean minced raw beef
4 rounded tsp Onion Bisto
1 large can (1¾lb or 794g) peeled tomatoes
1 level tsp garlic granules (or 1 crushed garlic clove)
3 rounded tsp salt
½ level tsp chili powder
1 level tsp oregano
4 rounded tbsp tomato purée
1 rounded tsp caster sugar
1 can (about 15¼oz or 432g) red kidney beans, drained

1 Place all ingredients except beans into large pan. Bring to boil, stirring.
2 Lower heat and cover. Simmer gently for 1 hour. Add beans. Reheat 10 to 15 minutes.
  Serve with rice and salad.

Chili Con Carne (serves 4)

This is how the Mexicans make a chili—and note that in the spelling there is only one l!

8oz (225g) well-washed kidney beans, soaked overnight in water to cover, then parboiled
1lb (500g) blade bone or chuck steak, cut into small
  cubes
1 bay leaf
4oz (125g) onion, very thinly sliced
1 large garlic clove, crushed
1 tbsp salad oil
8oz (225g) skinned tomatoes, chopped
1 level tsp salt
3 heaped tsp Bisto
2 level tsp cornflour
½ level tsp ground black pepper
½ level tsp oregano
¼ level tsp cumin
2 level tsp chili powder (*very* hot!)
¾pt (425ml) water

1 Place beans and water in which they were cooking into heavy-based pan. Add meat. Bring to boil, stirring.
2 Add bay leaf, onion and garlic. Lower heat and cover. Simmer about 1 hour or until beans and meat are *just* tender.
3 Pour oil into frying pan. Add all remaining ingredients. Bring to boil, stirring continuously. Simmer 5 minutes over minimal heat.
4 Stir into pan of beans and meat. Simmer a further 1 hour, when beans should be soft and meat tender. Stir from time to time to prevent chili catching over base of pan.

Serve with freshly cooked fluffy rice and a green salad.

Note
As salt has a toughening effect on beans, it should be added towards the latter part of cooking.

Viennese Onion Steaks (serves 4)

2oz (50g) butter
2 tsp salad oil
8oz (225g) onions, very thinly sliced
4 large 'flash-fry' or minute steaks
2 heaped tsp Bisto Rich Gravy Granules
1 tbsp cold water
¼pt (150ml) boiling water
salt and pepper to taste

1 Heat butter and oil in large frying pan. Add onions. Fry slowly until golden brown, allowing about 15 to 20 minutes.
2 Move to edges of pan. Add steaks. Fry until well-cooked and brown, turning once.
3 Meanwhile mix Bisto granules with cold water. Add boiling water, stirring.
4 Pour into pan over steak and onions. Stir round and cook gently until bubbling. Season to taste.
  Serve straight away with lightly fried potatoes (cooked first and sliced) and a green salad.

Austrian Soured-cream Beefsteaks (serves 4)

A special-occasion dish which teams happily with baby pasta and freshly cooked courgettes, lightly tossed in butter. Fried or grilled mushrooms can be served as well.

4 fairly thick rump or sirloin steaks, each 6oz (175g)
2oz (50g) butter
2 level tsp flour
2 level tsp Onion Bisto
½pt (275ml) water
1 rounded tbsp drained and finely chopped capers
3 rounded tbsp parsley
1 carton (5oz or 142ml) soured cream
salt and pepper to taste

1 Fry steaks in the butter according to taste (rare, medium or well-done). Remove from pan. Keep hot.
2 Stir flour and Bisto into rest of butter in pan. Gradually blend in water. Cook, stirring, until sauce comes to boil and thickens.
3 Stir in capers and parsley. Beat in cream, then season to taste. Bring just up to boil. Pour over steaks.
  Serve hot with suggested accompaniments.

Silverside—Hungarian Fashion (serves 8)

2oz (50g) lard or dripping
1lb (500g) onions, peeled and finely chopped
2 level tbsp paprika
1 level tsp caraway seeds
1 large garlic clove, crushed
½pt (275ml) tomato purée, made by blending skinned
   tomatoes in blender goblet
3 rounded tsp Bisto
4lb (2kg) unsalted silverside
salt and pepper to taste
water
8oz (225g) mushrooms, trimmed and sliced with
   stalks
8oz (225g) unsmoked bacon, cut into small cubes

1 Heat lard or dripping in large, flameproof casserole. Add onions. Cover pan. Fry over minimal heat till very pale and soft, about ½ hour.
2 Stir in paprika, caraway seeds, garlic, tomato purée and Bisto. Bring to a gentle boil, stirring continuously.
3 Add beef. Turn over and over in the onion and tomato mixture till well coated. Sprinkle with salt and pepper.
4 Add enough water to cover the meat halfway, then surround with mushrooms and bacon. Cover. Cook 3½ hours in oven set to 300°F (160°C), Gas 2.
5 Uncover and remove meat. Cut into thick slices and arrange on warm platter. Top with vegetables, etc, and sauce from pan.
   Accompany with boiled potatoes or small pasta.

Bulgarian Meat Balls in Egg and Yogurt Sauce (serves 4)

1lb (500g) raw minced beef, as lean as possible
2 rounded tsp Onion Bisto
1 × Grade 3 (standard) egg
½oz (15g) fresh white breadcrumbs
1 level tsp marjoram
salt and pepper to taste
½pt (275ml) boiling chicken stock (use cubes and
   water)
2 level tbsp long-grain rice
4 slightly rounded tbsp natural yogurt
1 egg yolk
1 level tsp cornflour

1 Combine beef with Bisto, egg, crumbs, marjoram and salt and pepper to taste.
2 With damp hands, shape into meat balls a little larger than walnuts.
3 Pour stock into pan. Add rice and meat balls. Lower heat. Cover. Simmer ½ hour.
4 To thicken, beat yogurt, egg yolk and cornflour well together. Season to taste. Stir into meat ball mixture.

5 Remove from heat as soon as sauce thickens.
   Serve with extra rice and a salad simply made from cucumber and tomatoes diced up, tossed with French dressing and garnished with grated Caerphilly cheese.

Turkish-style Stuffed Peppers (serves 4)

Stuffed peppers in Turkey, dished up straight from large and ferocious ovens, are packed with a genteel meat mixture which totally excludes rice; only the ones served cold contain the customary rice and copious quantities of oil.

4 medium green peppers (1lb or 500g)
boiling water
3oz (75g) onion
8oz (225g) raw minced beef
6oz (175g) skinned tomatoes, chopped
2 level tsp Bisto
¼ level tsp cinnamon
½ level tsp marjoram or basil
2oz (50g) button mushrooms, chopped
crumbs from 1 large slice white bread (crusts
   removed first)
½pt (275ml) tomato juice
4 tbsp water

1 Halve peppers. Remove inside seeds and fibrous portions. Stand halves upright in saucepan. Cover with boiling water. Simmer a few minutes until colour just begins to change from bright green to olive; no longer or peppers will fall apart.
2 Drain thoroughly by standing upside down on paper towels. Finely grate onion. Mix with all remaining ingredients except tomato juice and water.
3 Pack pepper halves with meat mixture. Stand in heatproof dish and coat with tomato juice and water, well mixed together. Bake, uncovered, for 25 to 30 minutes in oven set to 425°F (220°C), Gas 7.

   Serve hot as a first course, or as a main dish with extra vegetables and cooked rice.

Turkish-style Kebabs (serves 4)

1lb (500g) raw minced beef
2 level tsp Onion Bisto
1 large garlic clove, crushed
½ level tsp salt
½ level tsp ground cumin
3 level tsp parsley, very finely chopped

1 Mix beef thoroughly with all remaining ingredients. leave for 30 minutes.
2 Shape into 4 elongated patties and thread onto 4 longish skewers. (The patties should almost cover skewers.)
3 Grill about 8 minutes, turning frequently.

Serve with freshly cooked rice, or inside ovals of hollow pita bread. Accompany with yogurt and wedges of lemon. If liked, serve salad as well.

Russian-style Shichi (serves 4 to 6)

This is a complete meal of cabbage cream soup simmered gently with a piece of stewing beef such as shin. It is both filling and very appetising.

2lb (1kg) stewing steak in the piece (such as shin)
2 rounded tsp Bisto
2½pt (1½ litres) water
2 level tsp salt
2lb (1kg) Dutch white cabbage, finely shredded
8oz (225g) onions, finely chopped
1 can (about 16oz or 450g) tomatoes
pepper to taste
2 cartons (*each* 5oz or 142ml) soured cream

1 Put all ingredients, except cream, into a large pan. Bring to boil. Remove scum as it comes to top.
2 Lower heat. Cover. Simmer about 2½ hours when meat should be tender.
3 Take meat out of pan and cut into cubes. Return to soup. Bring to boil again. Remove from heat. Gradually beat in cream.

Serve piping hot with rye bread and butter.

Shichi main course beef
Remove beef from soup and keep hot. Serve soup as a first course with rye bread. Follow with cut-up beef accompanied by boiled potatoes, pickled beetroot and horseradish relish.

Russian-style shichi

Meaty minestrone

2 Lamb and Lamb Dishes

The delicate flavour of lamb is always a family favourite. Each cut is tender and can be cooked in a variety of ways and with sweet or savoury accompaniments. In May to October home-produced lamb is plentiful and in prime condition. For the rest of the year there is plenty of imported lamb. The forequarter of lamb (shoulder, scrag, middle and breast) is a good economical buy from May to October in particular. The other parts (chops and leg) are better bargains during winter and early spring.

Choosing and Buying Lamb

Lamb should have a fine-grained appearance and be moist, the colour being pinkish; the fat should be firm and white. Lamb which has aged too much is dark red in colour and has yellowish fat. Leg and shoulder should be plump with a paper-thin layer of skin covering the meat, and a bluish tinge on the knuckles.

Storing Lamb

Lamb can be kept for up to three days in the refrigerator. Place on a plate and cover lightly to prevent the colour fading. For fullest flavour, remove from the refrigerator in good time so that the meat is at room temperature when it starts cooking.

Cuts of Lamb

Breast
This cut is very cheap but inclined to be fatty. Boned, and with the surplus fat removed, however, breast of lamb makes an extremely tasty and economical cut for roasting.

Scrag end of neck
Usually cut into rounds, and suitable for soups and stews.

Middle neck
This is cut into chops, and can also be used for stews and casseroles.

Lamb fillet
This is the meat boned out of the whole neck into long fillets; ideal for grilling or oven roasting.

Best end of neck
This joint is the most versatile cut of lamb. It can be roasted whole or cut into cutlets for frying or grilling; boned and rolled and cut into slices called 'noisettes', or boned, rolled and stuffed as a roasting joint. For dinner parties the butcher can use two joints, each consisting of seven bones, and make a 'crown roast' or a 'guard of honour'.

Loin
The loin can be cut into loin chops or chump chops. The whole loin can be boned and stuffed as a rolled loin of lamb.

Shoulder
A cheaper joint than the leg with rather more fat, but considered to be tastier. The bone can be removed and the joint stuffed: this makes it go twice as far and also easier to carve. The shoulder is also divided into smaller joints: the blade and the knuckle end.

Leg
The prime and most popular joint of lamb for roasting. It can be bought whole or cut into the 'best end' and the 'knuckle end'. The best end can be roasted as a joint or boned to produce lamb cutlets. The shank or knuckle end is more popular and therefore more expensive.

Lamb's Liver and Kidneys

In addition to the main joints described above, lamb also provides delicious liver and kidneys, both highly nutritious for family meals. See Section 6, page 110.

Liver
Liver should be washed and dried, and any gristly substance removed. It can be grilled, fried or baked, covered with a layer of stuffing.

Kidneys
Kidneys should have fat and skin removed and the white core cut out with a sharp pair of scissors (it is easier to do this if the kidney is cut in half first). Kidneys are delicious grilled, fried with bacon, or used to stuff baked jacket potatoes for supper. To do this, scrub the potatoes and cut in half; hollow out a little from both halves, then put in the kidney and sprinkle it with pepper and salt. Re-form the potato, wrap the whole in foil and bake for the usual time. Serve with a knob of butter.

Roast Lamb

Choose your joint for roasting, referring to the list of cuts given below. Roast for 25 minutes per pound (500g) plus 25 minutes at 375°F (190°C), Gas 5. Serve with extra roast or boiled potatoes, peas and/or carrots, redcurrant jelly or mint sauce, and Bisto gravy.

In general, the amounts to allow per person are:

8 to 12oz (225 to 350g) lamb with bone
4 to 6oz (125 to 175g) lamb without bone

Freezing

Made-up lamb dishes, or pieces of cooked lamb, may be frozen for up to six months.

Glazed Loin of Lamb (serves 4 to 6)

A beautiful partnership between the delicate flavour of lamb and the tanginess of the redcurrant-jelly glaze.

2lb (1kg) loin of lamb (in one piece)

Glaze
2 rounded tbsp redcurrant jelly
1 rounded tbsp thick honey
1 tbsp lemon juice

Garnish
1 medium cooking apple
2 level tbsp granulated sugar
4 tbsp water
redcurrant jelly
sprigs of mint

1 Score surface of lamb, in diamond pattern, with a sharp knife, as this enables the glaze to penetrate more readily.
2 Place meat in small roasting tin. For glaze, put all ingredients into pan. Stir over low heat until jelly has melted.
3 Brush scored area of joint heavily with glaze. Roast 1¼ to 1½ hours in oven set to 350°F (180°C), Gas 4. Brush with more glaze while the joint is roasting and continue till all the glaze is used up.
4 About 15 to 20 minutes before lamb is ready, peel and core apple, cut it into rings and halve each.
5 Put sugar and water into pan. Stir over low heat till dissolved. Add halved apple slices. Cover. Cook gently about 5 to 6 minutes.

To serve, stand the meat on a warm serving dish and garnish with a border of drained apple slices. Top apples with a little redcurrant jelly, then add sprigs of mint. Accompany with roast or new potatoes, peas and Bisto gravy.

The cuts of lamb:
1 *chump chops* **2** *fillet or best end of leg* **3** *shank or knuckle end of leg* **4** *best end chops* **5** *best end of neck* **6** *loin chops* **7** *loin* **8** *scrag end of neck* **9** *middle neck* **10** *shoulder* **11** *breast* **12** *lamb fillet*

Carving Lamb

Shoulder

Start carving with the crisp side of the skin uppermost, and cut a long thick slice from the centre of the joint right down to the bone. (With this joint you will find it easiest to use a cloth to hold the shank end of the joint.) Then cut slices from both sides of your first incision until you have carved all of the centre wedge. Now turn the joint over, so that you can carve the meat from the shank bone. When you have finished carving the shank, turn the joint over again and, carving horizontally, remove the remainder of the meat from the bone.

Loin

If your joint is boned, rolled or stuffed, you simply carve it vertically, in rather thicker slices than you would cut beef. If the joint is on the bone, remove the chine bone first, then carve vertically downwards. The natural division of the bones will help you to cut the joint into thick slices or chops.

Leg

Turn the thickest side of the joint uppermost and carve out two slices from the middle of the leg, cutting right down to the bone. These should be fairly thick slices, say ¼ inch (1cm). Then continue slicing from both sides. The remaining meat, on the other side of the joint, should be carved horizontally. Again you will find all this easier if you use a cloth to hold the shank end while you carve.

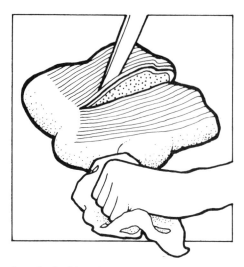

Cut from both sides of the first slice

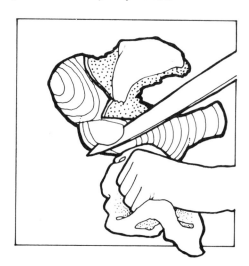

Turn over and carve from the shank bone

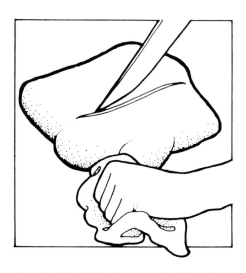

Carving shoulder of lamb: cut a slice from the centre

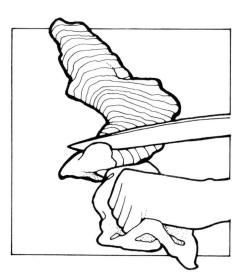

Turn back again and carve horizontally

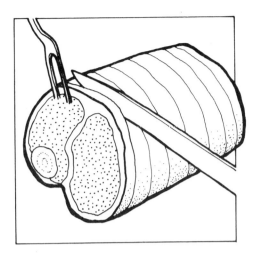

Carving loin of lamb

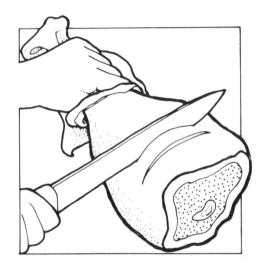

Carving leg: cut 2 slices from the middle

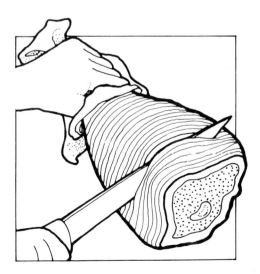

Then cut from each side of these

Lamb and Bean Hotpot (serves 4)

4oz (100 to 125g) haricot beans, soaked overnight,
  then parboiled
4oz (100 to 125g) red kidney beans, soaked overnight,
  then parboiled
4 pieces scrag-end neck of lamb
2 tbsp salad oil
1 large onion, thinly sliced
salt and pepper to taste
1 bouquet garni
4 heaped tsp Bisto
¾pt (425ml) water
toasted breadcrumbs or crispy fried-onion rings

1 Drain beans and leave on one side temporarily.
2 Trim away and discard excess fat from lamb.
3 Heat oil in a fairly shallow pan until hot. Add lamb. Fry on both sides until golden brown. Drain on paper towels.
4 Arrange alternate layers of beans, lamb and onion in ovenproof casserole, sprinkling salt and pepper lightly between layers. Add bouquet garni.
5 Mix Bisto to a smooth cream with some of the water. Blend in rest of water. Pour into casserole.
6 Cover with lid or foil. Cook for 3½ hours in cool oven set to 300°F (150°C), Gas 3. Uncover. Remove bouquet garni. Sprinkle top with crumbs or onion rings.

Serve with mashed parsnips and cabbage or peas.

Crown roast of lamb

Crown Roast of Lamb (serves 6)

A spectacular way of presenting lamb—but enlist the help of your butcher well in advance.

1 crown of lamb
nut and apricot stuffing (see recipe below)
1oz (25g) butter or margarine, melted
halved glacé cherries
cutlet frills

1 Advise your butcher that you would like him to prepare a crown from two best-end necks of lamb, each with 6 cutlets.
2 If you are forced to prepare the roast yourself, buy two already-chined best-end necks of lamb.
3 To separate cutlets, cut in between bones, stopping about halfway down each. Scrape fat from upper part of bones, leaving about 3 inches (7½cm) bare.
4 With skin side outside, curve both necks round to form a crown and hold together by stitching both ends with thick thread.
5 Stand in roasting tin and fill centre with stuffing. Cover ends of bones with pieces of foil to prevent burning. Brush with butter or margarine and roast 2¼ to 2½ hours (or until golden-brown and cooked through) in oven set to 325°F (160°C), Gas 3.
6 Transfer the crown to your carving board. Remove foil from ends of bones and replace with alternate halved cherries and cutlet frills.
  Serve with gravy made from Bisto Rich Gravy Granules. Accompany with roast and boiled potatoes and sprouts.

Nut and apricot stuffing
4oz (125g) fresh white breadcrumbs
2oz (50g) dried apricots, soaked overnight and snipped into small pieces
2oz (50g) onion, finely grated
1oz (25g) walnuts, finely chopped
½ level tsp finely grated orange peel
½ level tsp basil
1 × Grade 3 (standard) egg, beaten
cold milk
salt and pepper to taste

1 Put first six ingredients into bowl. Bind fairly loosely with beaten egg and milk.
2 Season to taste and use as required.

Crown Roast with Cauliflower (serves 6)

For slimmers, omit the breadcrumb stuffing. After the crown has been removed from the oven, fill its centre with a freshly cooked cauliflower. Decorate the tops of the bones as directed.

Guard of Honour (serves 6)

Another impressive lamb roast, also made from two best-end necks of lamb with 6 or 7 cutlets on each. Ask the butcher to chine the necks, then stand both pieces together, skin side outside, so that the bones cross in the centre. Hold in place by tying bones together with string where they cross. Pack with stuffing, protect the bones, baste with 1oz (25g) melted butter and roast as for crown roast of lamb (above). Top bones with cutlet frills and serve with assorted vegetables and gravy made from Bisto Rich Gravy Granules.

Souffled shepherd's casserole

Rack of Lamb (serves 3 to 4)

Popular in America, this consists of 1 best-end neck of lamb (with 7 to 8 cutlets) roasted in the piece. Chine the joint and clean the bones, as given in the recipe for crown roast lamb (above). Stand the joint in a roasting tin so that it is upright with the fat either on the left or the right. Sprinkle lightly with garlic salt and crushed rosemary. Roast about 1¼ to 1½ hours in oven set to 325°F (190°C), Gas 5. Serve with mixed vegetables and gravy made from Bisto Rich Gravy Granules.

Party Lamb Roast (serves 8 to 10)

4lb (2kg) leg of lamb, boned out by the butcher

Stuffing
2oz (50g) onion
2oz (50g) Brazil nuts
1oz (25g) parsley, chopped
1 can (about 15oz or 425g) apricot halves, drained and coarsely chopped
4oz (100 to 125g) fresh white breadcrumbs
2 level tsp Bisto
1 tsp lemon juice
1 × Grade 3 (standard) egg, beaten
2oz (50g) butter or dripping, melted

1 Wash and dry lamb. Cut away and discard surplus fat.
2 To make stuffing, finely grate onion and thinly slice nuts. Put both into bowl. Add parsley, chopped apricots, crumbs, Bisto and lemon juice.
3 Bind to a stuffing with the egg and half the butter or dripping.
4 Pack fairly loosely into meat cavity. Tie into shape with string or alternatively secure with skewers. Stand on rack in roasting tin.
5 Brush rest of butter or dripping over meat. Roast, uncovered, 2½ hours in oven set to 350°F (180°C), Gas 4.

Carve fairly thickly and serve with roast potatoes, mangetout or sliced green beans, apple sauce and gravy made from Bisto Rich Gravy Granules and pan juices.

Note
Reserve apricot syrup from can and use in milk shakes, mousses, sauces, etc.

Haricot Lamb (serves 6)

4oz (125g) haricot beans, soaked overnight
1½lb (750g) boned shoulder of lamb (boned weight)
1oz (25g) butter or margarine
2 tsp salad oil
8oz (225g) onions, chopped
4oz (125g) carrots, thinly sliced
3 heaped tsp Bisto

¾pt (425ml) water
1 level tsp mixed herbs
4oz (125g) skinned tomatoes, chopped
salt and pepper to taste

1 Drain beans. Leave on one side temporarily. Dice meat, removing as much surplus fat as possible.
2 Heat butter or margarine and oil in heavy pan. Add lamb, a little at a time. Fry briskly till well-sealed and golden. Remove to plate.
3 Add onions and carrots to pan. Fry till golden. Stir in Bisto and water. Bring to boil, stirring.
4 Add lamb, beans, herbs and tomatoes. Season. Mix well. Bring to boil. Skim. Lower heat.
5 Cover pan and simmer gently for 2 to 2¼ hours or until beans and lamb are tender.

Serve with green vegetables and boiled potatoes.

Stuffed Lamb Pocket with Calvados Sauce (serves 8)

1lb (500g) raw lean minced beef
1 level tsp dried rosemary, crumbled between finger and thumb
1 × grade 2 (large) egg, beaten
2 level tsp Onion Bisto
2 large garlic cloves, crushed
1 × 4lb (2kg) lamb shoulder (boned weight)
1oz (25g) butter, melted

Gravy
4 heaped tsp Bisto
¾pt (425ml) water
3 tbsp Calvados (French apple brandy)

1 For stuffing, combine meat with rosemary, egg, Bisto and garlic.
2 Pack it into the lamb (there will be a gap left from boning), and hold edges of meat together by sewing with double thickness of thread.
3 Stand in roasting tin and brush with butter. Place in hot oven set to 425°F (220°C), Gas 7. Reduce temperature to 375°F (190°C), Gas 5. Roast 2 hours, basting occasionally.
4 Stand meat on a board and keep hot. For gravy, pour off all but 2 tbsp fat from roasting tin. Stand tin over medium heat.
5 Stir in Bisto and water. Bring to boil, stirring continuously. Heat Calvados to lukewarm. Set alight. Pour into gravy. Stir in well. Adjust seasoning to taste.
6 Remove thread from lamb. Carve.

Serve with gravy, roast potatoes and spinach or peas.

Glazed loin of lamb

Easy Shepherd's Pie (serves 4)

12oz (350g) cold cooked lamb, finely minced
½pt (275ml) gravy, made with Bisto Rich Gravy
   Granules as directed
onion salt to taste
1lb (500g) freshly boiled potatoes
1oz (25g) butter
a few tbsp milk
salt and pepper to taste

1 Combine lamb, gravy and onion salt together. Transfer to a 2½ pint (1½ litre) greased heatproof dish. Leave until a skin forms on the top—about 10 minutes.
2 Mash potatoes finely. Beat in butter and milk. Season to taste with salt and pepper. Spread over meat mixture.
3 Ridge potatoes with a fork and bake ½ hour at 425°F (220°C), Gas 7.
   Serve hot with green vegetables.

Summer Lamb Hotpot (serves 4)

8 lamb chops, cut from best end of neck
1 level tbsp flour mixed with 3 rounded tsp Bisto
1 tbsp salad oil
8oz (225g) skinned tomatoes, sliced
1 tsp Worcestershire sauce
2 level tsp bottled mint sauce
1 bunch spring onions, trimmed but left whole
8oz (225g) runner beans, side strings removed, sliced
4oz (100 to 125g) green peas (shelled weight)
4oz (100 to 125g) new carrots, scraped, left whole
1lb (500g) new potatoes, scraped, left whole
½pt (275ml) water

1 Trim chops, removing excess fat. Coat liberally with flour and Bisto mixture.
2 Heat oil in shallow frying pan. Add chops. Fry until golden on both sides.
3 Fill 4pt (2¼ litre) casserole with all the ingredients, making sure 4 chops are at the base of the dish and 4 are on top.
4 Cover. Cook 1½ hours in oven set to 375°F (190°C), Gas 5.
 Serve hot and allow 2 chops per person.

Lancashire Hotpot (serves 4 to 6)

1½lb (750g) middle neck of lamb, cut into even-sized pieces
2 medium onions, sliced
1lb (500g) potatoes, peeled and sliced
salt and pepper to taste
4 heaped tsp Bisto
¾pt (425ml) water
1½oz (40g) butter or margarine

1 Arrange the meat and vegetables in layers in a casserole, seasoning each layer. Finish with a layer of potatoes.
2 Blend the Bisto to a smooth paste with a little of the water. Add remaining water.
3 Pour the Bisto liquid into the casserole. Dot the surface with small knobs of butter or margarine.
4 Cover the casserole and cook 2½ hours at 300°F (150°C), Gas 2. Remove lid and increase oven heat to 375°F (190°C), Gas 5, for ½ hour to brown the top layer of potatoes.

Lancashire Hotpot with Kidney (serves 4 to 6)
Make as above but include 2 sliced lamb's kidneys as an extra.

Curried Lamb Hotpot (serves 4 to 6)

A speedily-prepared dish with a fine flavour; a good choice for midweek.

1½lb (750g) middle neck of lamb
1oz (25g) margarine
16oz (450g) turnips
1 medium onion, peeled and chopped
1 level tbsp plain flour
2 level tsp Bisto
1 level tbsp curry powder
salt and pepper to taste
water
2oz (50g) sultanas
chopped parsley for garnishing

1 Trim lamb, removing excess fat. Melt margarine in frying pan. Add lamb. Fry meat briskly until brown on all sides. Transfer to 4 pint (2¼ litre) casserole.
2 Cut turnips into smallish chunks. Add to pan of remaining margarine with onion. Fry about 5 minutes, keeping heat low to prevent vegetables from browning too much.
3 Put flour, Bisto, curry powder and salt and pepper to taste into measuring cup. Mix to a smooth paste with a little cold water. Make up to ½pt (275ml) with extra water.
4 Pour into frying pan and combine with vegetables. Add sultanas. Bring slowly to boil, stirring continuously.
5 Ladle over lamb in casserole. Cover. Cook 1½ to 1¾ hours in oven set to 350°F (180°C), Gas 4. Sprinkle heavily with parsley.
 Serve with freshly boiled rice and mango chutney.

Irish-style Stew (serves 4)

2lb (1kg) potatoes, peeled and thinly sliced
12oz (350g) onions, thinly sliced
2lb (1kg) middle neck of lamb
2 rounded tsp Bisto
¾pt (425ml) water
salt and pepper to taste
2 heaped tbsp chopped parsley

1 Fill a large pan with alternate layers of potatoes, onions and lamb.
2 Mix Bisto to a smooth paste with a little water. Blend in rest of water. Season to taste.
3 Pour into pan. Cover. Simmer gently for 1½ hours when lamb should be tender.

Serve piping hot and sprinkle each serving with parsley.

Lamb and Potato Bake (serves 4)

1 rounded tbsp plain flour
¼ level tsp dried rosemary, crushed between finger and thumb
1 level tsp salt
shake of pepper
1½lb (750g) potatoes, very thinly sliced
1 medium onion, peeled and thinly sliced
2 level tsp Bisto
water
4 lamb chump chops
sprigs of parsley for garnishing

1 Mix together flour, rosemary, salt and pepper. Arrange alternate layers of potatoes and onions in 3pt (1¾ litre) casserole. Begin and end with potatoes, and sprinkle flour mix between layers.
2 Put Bisto into measuring cup. Mix smoothly with a little cold water. Make up to ½pt (275ml) with extra water. Pour into casserole over potatoes and onions.
3 Arrange chops on top. Cook, uncovered, for 1 hour in oven set to 375°F (190°C), Gas 5. Garnish with parsley.

Serve with a crunchy salad such as coleslaw.

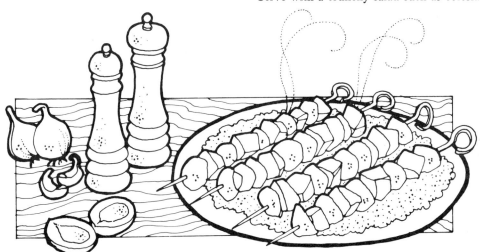

Lamb and apricot kebabs

Lamb and Apricot Kebabs (serves 8)

8oz (225g) dried apricots, soaked overnight
2¼ to 2½lb (1 to 1¼kg) lamb fillet
4oz (125g) onion, finely grated
2 large garlic cloves, crushed
½ level tsp salt
10oz (275g) natural yogurt
½ level tsp ground cardamom
2 heaped tsp Bisto Rich Gravy Granules
3 tsp boiling water

1 Drain apricots. Cut lamb fillet (fat-trimmed first) into 1 inch (2½cm) pieces. Thread on to 8 skewers with halved apricots.

2 Mix together onion, garlic, salt, yogurt and cardamom. Stir in Bisto granules mixed with the boiling water.
3 Stand kebabs on a large plate. Coat with yogurt mixture by spooning equal amounts over each. Turn over. Coat second side of kebabs with rest of yogurt mixture.
4 Leave in the refrigerator, uncovered, for 2 hours. Brush once again with yogurt mixture, then grill under high heat about 15 minutes, turning twice.

Serve with freshly cooked rice and green peas. If any yogurt mixture is left over, spoon into a bowl and serve as a sauce with the kebabs.

Spicy Lamb (serves 4)

1½lb (750g) lamb fillet
1oz (25g) butter or margarine
2 medium onions
1 large garlic clove, crushed
1 rounded tbsp plain flour
1 rounded tbsp tomato purée
2 level tsp Bisto
½pt (275ml) water
½ level tsp salt
pepper to taste
½ level tsp cumin seed
¼ level tsp ground allspice

1 Cut meat into 1 inch (2½cm) cubes. Heat butter or margarine in pan. Add meat, onions and garlic. Fry over medium heat for 5 minutes, turning.
2 Add all remaining ingredients and bring to boil, stirring. Transfer to ovenproof casserole. Cover. Cook 1 to 1¼ hours in oven set to 350°F (180°C), Gas 4.
   Serve with creamy mashed potatoes and a crunchy salad made with Chinese leaves, celery, sliced onions and sliced oranges.

Sweet Lamb Casserole (serves 4 to 6)

3lb (1½kg) boned breast of lamb, rolled and tied
2 medium onions, sliced
1oz (25g) butter or margarine
1 tbsp salad oil
1oz (25g) seedless raisins
1oz (25g) currants
finely grated peel of 1 medium orange
4 heaped tsp Bisto
1pt (575ml) water
salt and pepper
3 rosy-skinned eating apples, unpeeled, cored and sliced

1 Cut between string of lamb to give fairly thick slices or noisettes.
2 Fry lamb with onions in the butter or margarine and salad oil for 5 minutes.
3 Transfer to ovenproof casserole. Add raisins, currants and orange peel.
4 Blend Bisto to a smooth paste with a little of the cold water. Add rest of water.
5 Pour into casserole. Season to taste by sprinkling with salt and pepper.
6 Cover. Cook 1 hour in oven set to 350°F (180°C), Gas 4. Remove from oven, uncover and arrange apple rings on top.
7 Cover again and cook for a further ½ hour.
   Serve with rice, pasta or creamed potatoes. Accompany with green vegetables to taste.

Lamb Rosemary (serves 4)

4 pieces scrag-end neck of lamb
1 level tbsp flour seasoned with salt and pepper
1 large onion, sliced
3 tbsp salad oil
4 rounded tsp Bisto
1pt (575ml) water
1 level tsp rosemary, crushed between finger and thumb
3 medium celery stalks, thinly sliced
4oz (100 to 125g) button mushrooms, trimmed

1 Dust the lamb in seasoned flour.
2 Fry the onion in the oil for 3 minutes. Add the lamb and fry until browned on all sides.
3 Blend the Bisto to a smooth paste with a little of the water. Add the remaining water.
4 Stir the Bisto liquid into the meat. Add the rosemary, celery and mushrooms.
5 Cover the pan and simmer gently for 1½ hours.
   Serve with baked jacket potatoes and spinach or cabbage.

Greek Stifado with Lamb (serves 6)

A classic Greek stew that can also be made with chicken, rabbit, hare or beef.

4 tbsp salad oil
6oz (175g) onion, chopped
3 to 6 garlic cloves, crushed (quantity to taste)
2lb (1kg) boned shoulder of lamb (boned weight), cubed
3 heaped tsp Bisto
¼pt (150ml) tomato juice
2 rounded tbsp tomato purée
¼pt (150ml) dry red wine
2 level tsp sugar
salt and pepper to taste
12 to 16 pickled onions (mild variety, and optional)

1 Heat oil in heavy pan. Add onion. Fry gently till pale gold. Add garlic and meat cubes. Fry briskly until well-sealed and golden brown.
2 Stir in Bisto followed by next 4 ingredients. Bring to boil, stirring. Lower heat. Season. Cover.
3 Simmer gently for 1½ to 2 hours or until meat is tender. Stir from time to time to prevent sticking.
   Serve with boiled potatoes and green vegetables to taste.

Lamb and bean hotpot

Scotch broth

Scotch Broth (serves 6 to 8)

A complete meal, Scotch broth is a marvellous winter warmer and less expensive than many meat dishes.

1½lb (750g) scrag-end neck of lamb, trimmed of
    surplus fat and cut up into small pieces
3 heaped tsp Bisto
6oz (175g) onions, chopped
8oz (225g) mixed root vegetables (turnip, swede and
    parsnip) diced
3oz (75g) carrots, diced
6oz (175g) potatoes, diced
2 medium celery stalks, sliced
2oz (50g) pearl barley
3pt (about 1¾ litres) water
2 to 3 level tsp salt

1 Toss meat in Bisto. Transfer to large pan. Add all remaining ingredients.
2 Slowly bring to boil, stirring. Lower heat. Skim.
3 Cover. Simmer gently about 1½ hours, stirring from time to time.
    Serve very hot with crusty brown bread.

Curried Lamb Soup (serves 4)

12oz (350g) scrag-end neck of lamb
2 tbsp salad oil
1 large onion, chopped
1 large garlic clove, chopped
1 level tbsp mild Madras curry powder
4 level tsp Bisto
1pt (575ml) water
1 can (8oz or 225g) tomatoes
1 medium dessert apple, peeled, cored and chopped
1oz (25g) seedless raisins
2 level tbsp chutney (such as mango)
salt and pepper to taste

1 Cut lamb into small pieces, discarding bone and removing any excess fat.
2 Heat oil in fairly large pan. Add lamb, onion and garlic. Fry about 7 to 8 minutes, turning.
3 Stir in curry powder and cook a further minute. Mix Bisto to a smooth paste with a little of the cold water. Add rest of water.
4 Pour into pan over meat and onion mixture. Add tomatoes. Stir well to mix. Bring to boil. Lower heat. Cover.
5 Add apples, raisins and chutney. Simmer, covered, a further ½ hour when lamb should be tender. Adjust seasoning to taste.
    Serve with freshly cooked Basmati rice and side dishes (sambals) of tomato and onion salad, batter-coated and deep-fried onion rings, chutney and a bowl of natural yogurt. Popadams may be included as well.

Tip
This is a substantial soup and makes a warming and sustaining main course for lunch or supper.

Lamb Moussaka (serves 4)

Best with cooked lamb, this is an appetising Greek speciality which can be economically made with the remains of the weekend joint.

12oz (350g) cold cooked lamb
½oz (15g) butter or margarine
1 medium onion, coarsely grated
1 rounded tsp Bisto
½ level tsp marjoram
salt and pepper to taste
1 can (14oz or 400g) tomatoes
1½lb (750g) parboiled potatoes, sliced

Sauce
½pt (275ml) freshly made white sauce
2oz (50g) Cheddar cheese finely grated
1 × Grade 3 (standard) egg, beaten

1 Mince lamb. Heat butter or margarine in pan. Add onion. Fry gently until light gold.
2 Stir in lamb, Bisto, marjoram and seasoning to taste. Drain tomatoes and coarsely chop. Reserve liquor from can.
3 Fill a 4 pint (2¼ litres) ovenproof casserole with alternate layers of potatoes, meat mixture and chopped tomatoes, beginning and ending with potatoes.
4 Pour tomato liquor over the top. Leave to stand 5 minutes. Meanwhile, place sauce over a low heat. Add cheese and stir until melted.
5 Blend egg into sauce, adjust seasoning to taste and pour over potatoes. Cover with lid or foil and cook ¾ hour in oven set to 375°F (190°C), Gas 5. Uncover. Continue to cook further ½ hour or until top is golden.
Serve hot with a mixed salad.

Balkan Lamb Balls in Caraway Sauce (serves 6 to 8)

With exotica creeping in, this is a splendid dish to keep in reserve for special occasions. Serve with freshly cooked rice and a crisp green salad.

1½lb (750g) minced lamb (best cut is top part of leg)
3oz (75g) plain flour
3 heaped tsp Onion Bisto
1 × Grade 3 (standard) egg, well beaten
salt and pepper to taste

Sauce
4 × Grade 3 (standard) eggs
12oz (350g) natural yogurt
2 level tsp cornflour
1 level tsp caraway seeds, crushed in electric grinder or with pestle and mortar
salt and pepper to taste

1 Brush a shallow roasting tin heavily with melted lard. Dust with flour.
2 Mix lamb with all remaining ingredients. Shape into balls no larger than walnuts. Stand in roasting tin. Bake ½ hour in oven set to 375°F (190°C), Gas 5. Do not cover.
3 Transfer to a heatproof casserole which is shallow rather than deep. Beat together all sauce ingredients and cook over a low heat until mixture *just* comes up to the boil and thickens.
4 Pour over lamb balls. Return to oven. Cover. Cook 20 minutes.
Serve with pasta and green vegetables.

Alpine-style Lamb Hotpot (serves 6 to 8)

4lb (2kg) leg of lamb, fat trimmed off as much as possible
1oz (25g) plain flour, mixed with 3 heaped tsp Onion Bisto
1oz (25g) bacon dripping or butter
1lb (500g) potatoes, coarsely diced
8oz (225g) carrots, thickly sliced
1 small celeriac, thickly peeled and cut into tiny dice
1 large garlic clove, crushed
¼pt (150ml) dry red wine
¼pt (150ml) water

1 Coat meat heavily with flour-and-Bisto mixture. Heat dripping or butter in large flameproof casserole. Add lamb.
2 Fry until golden-brown and well-sealed all over, turning frequently with 2 spoons. Add all remaining ingredients.
3 Cover closely with lid or foil. Cook 2 hours in oven set to 350°F (180°C), Gas 4.
To serve, carve into thickish slices and accompany with vegetables and gravy from pan.

Kebab-Shoppe-style from Bulgaria (serves 4)

A feast of a meal, this is a luxury minted lamb stew from the Balkans, thickened with eggs and yogurt—in the same way as the Bulgarian meat balls on page 37.

1½lb (750g) leg of lamb, boned weight and diced
6oz (175g) skinned tomatoes, chopped
4oz (100 to 125g) onions, peeled and chopped
1 level tsp paprika
1 level tsp salt
2oz (50g) butter, melted
1 level tsp marjoram
2 chilies, washed but left whole (don't eat, as the inner seeds are like fire!)
4 tbsp water
2 rounded tsp Bisto
1 carton (5oz or 142ml) natural yogurt
2 × Grade 4 (small) eggs
1 level tbsp fresh mint, very finely chopped

1 Place all ingredients, except last 5, into large saucepan. Bring to boil. Skim. Stir round.
2 Lower heat. Cover. Simmer gently about 1½ hours or until lamb is tender, adding a little water if mixture seems to be drying out.
3 To thicken, beat water, Bisto, yogurt, eggs and mint well together. Pour into pan. Bring just up to boil. Remove at once from heat.

Serve with rice, and either grilled or fried mushrooms which is traditional. Otherwise accompany with bread.

Lamb Guvetch (serves 6 to 8)

Probably *the* national dish of Bulgaria, guvetch is a glorious conglomeration of assorted summer vegetables simmered slowly with lamb. It is usually eaten with rice.

3lb (1½kg) middle neck of lamb
4 tbsp salad oil
1lb (500g) onions, chopped
2 large garlic cloves, crushed
2lb (1kg) red or green peppers (or mixture), de-seeded and cut into strips
1lb (500g) French beans, trimmed and halved
1lb (500g) tomatoes, skinned and chopped
3 rounded tsp Bisto
¼ to ½ level tsp cayenne pepper (hot, so be very careful!)
salt to taste

1 Ask butcher to chop up lamb into 2 inch (5cm) pieces. Wash and dry. Cut away excess fat.
2 Heat oil in large pan. Add onions, garlic and peppers. Fry gently, with lid on pan, about ½ hour or until vegetables are soft.

3 Stir in all remaining ingredients, including lamb. Slowly bring to boil, stirring. Cover. Simmer 1½ to 2 hours, when meat should be very tender and gravy thick. Stir occasionally to prevent sticking.

Moroccan Chick Pea and Lamb Stew (serves 4 to 6)

2lb (1kg) middle neck of lamb, cut into neat pieces
2 tbsp salad oil
4 to 5oz (125g) onions, finely chopped
2 level tbsp flour
3 heaped tsp Bisto
½ level tsp ground ginger
½ level tsp mixed spice
1½pt (just under 1 litre) hot water
1 medium washed and unpeeled aubergine, sliced then coarsely diced
1 medium green pepper, de-seeded and cut into strips
3 large tomatoes, skinned and quartered
6oz (175g) chick peas, soaked overnight, then drained
salt and pepper to taste

1 Wash lamb and dry with paper towels.
2 Heat oil in large and heavy-based pan. Add onions. Cover. Fry gently until pale gold. Move to one side of pan.
3 Add lamb. Fry a little more briskly until pieces are well-sealed and golden-brown.
4 Stir in flour, Bisto, ginger and spice. Gradually blend in water. Bring gently to boil, turning meat over and over.
5 Add all remaining ingredients. Reduce heat till mixture bubbles gently. Cover. Simmer for about 1½ to 1¾ hours, when both lamb and chick peas should be tender.

Serve with freshly boiled rice and a green salad.

Spicy lamb

Lamb Stewed in Turkish Fashion (serves 4)

2 tbsp salad or olive oil
8oz (225g) onions, chopped
1 garlic clove, crushed
6oz (175g) carrots, cut into ½ inch (1¼cm) slices
1lb (500g) leg of lamb (boned weight) cut into cubes
3 rounded tsp Bisto
¼pt (150ml) water
2 tbsp tomato purée
1 medium red pepper (green if red not available)
bouquet garni
½ large lemon, very thinly sliced
1lb (500g) peeled potatoes, washed and halved
8oz (225g) pre-cooked butter beans (either cooked yourself or canned)

1 Heat oil in large pan. Add onions and garlic. Fry gently until pale gold. Add carrots. Toss round in the oil with the onions and garlic.

2 Add meat, a few pieces at a time. Fry briskly until sealed and deep gold. Stir in Bisto.

3 Gradually blend in water. Cook, stirring, until mixture comes to boil and thickens. Add all remaining ingredients except potatoes and beans. Cover. Simmer 1½ hours.

4 Add potatoes. Cover again. Cook a further ¼ hour. Stir in beans (drained if canned). Simmer 10 minutes.

Serve with green vegetables.

Madras Lamb Curry (serves 4)

1 large onion, chopped
1 medium green pepper, de-seeded and chopped
2 chilies, de-seeded and finely chopped (or stir in
  1 level tsp cayenne pepper with lemon juice)
2 large garlic cloves, crushed
3 tbsp salad oil
2 rounded tbsp Madras curry powder
1lb (500g) leg of lamb, boned and diced
3 heaped tsp Bisto
½pt (275ml) water
2 rounded tsp tomato purée
juice of 1 medium lemon

1 Gently fry onion, pepper, chilies and garlic in oil
for 4 minutes.
2 Add the curry powder and continue cooking for a
further 2 to 3 minutes.
3 Add cubed meat and fry until lightly browned.
4 Mix Bisto to a smooth paste with a little of the
water. Blend in remaining water, tomato purée and
lemon juice.
5 Bring to the boil, cover and simmer for 2 hours or
until the meat is tender.
6 Garnish with lemon wedges, apple quarters,
banana slices or sliced peppers.
  Serve with rice, popadams and chutney.

South African Lamb Bobotie (serves 4)

2 large slices white bread (crusts left on)
¼pt (150ml) cold milk
1 large onion
2 tsp salad oil
1lb (500g) boned shoulder of lamb, minced
1 level tbsp Madras curry powder
3 rounded tsp Bisto
2 level tsp soft brown sugar
1 tbsp mild malt or cider vinegar
2oz (50g) currants, raisins or sultanas (or mixture)
1oz (25g) Brazil nuts, cut into wafer-thin slivers
salt and pepper to taste
2 × Grade 3 (standard) eggs

1 Dice bread. Place in bowl. Add half the milk.
Leave on one side temporarily.
2 Cut onion into very thin slices. Separate slices into
rings. Heat oil in sturdy pan. Add onion. Fry gently
until pale gold. Stir in lamb.
3 Increase heat. Fry a little more briskly till meat is
brown and crumbly, breaking it up with a fork all the
time.
4 Stir in next 6 ingredients. Add bread, first finely
mashed up in milk in which it was soaking. Season.
Beat in 1 egg. Combine with meat mixture.
5 Spread into greased 2 pint (about 1¼ litre)
casserole. Beat rest of milk and last egg well together.
Pour over meat mixture.
6 Bake 1¼ hours in cool oven set to 325°F (160°C),
Gas 3.
Serve hot with green vegetables to taste and sliced
carrots tossed in butter.

Note
This dish is fairly substantial and therefore rice, pasta
or potatoes should be unnecessary.

Madras lamb curry

3 Pork, Bacon and Ham

Nowadays pork can be eaten at any time of year. It should always be thoroughly cooked, but can be served in numerous ways, both hot and cold. Shoulder, hand and spring, and belly are the economical cuts; they can be used to make pies, casseroles and stews, as well as for roasting.

Choosing and Buying Pork

The flesh should be finely grained and pinkish in colour. The fat should be firm and creamy-white. Pork that has been subjected to too much refrigerator chilling is brownish in colour, damp or sticky to touch, with fat that is soft and grey.

Storing Pork

Pork should be put in the refrigerator on a plate and covered lightly to prevent drying out. Do not place fresh meat in the frozen food section of the refrigerator—use this only for meat already frozen.

Cuts of Pork

Leg

This is a prime joint, usually sold divided into two smaller joints—knuckle and fillet, or best end of leg. Both are ideal for roasting. The knuckle end can be boned, stuffed and roasted. Slices cut from the boned fillet or best end of leg can be grilled or fried to make a delicious meal.

Belly

This is an inexpensive joint, which is usually boned and rolled for roasting. Belly can be divided into thick and thin end. Sliced belly cut into thick rashers is excellent for an economical meal, served grilled or fried. Belly is often salted in brine and then boned, boiled and pressed for serving cold. It can also be braised or stewed. The Chinese cut 'spare ribs' are the rib bones from the boned belly, and should not be confused with spare rib chops, which come from the shoulder.

Loin

The loin of pork is divided into chump, middle and best or rib end of loin. The chump and middle loin can be roasted whole or cut into chops which can be fried, grilled or baked. Best rib end of loin is usually sold as chops for grilling or frying. Pork tenderloin or fillet is the lean, thin piece of meat cut from the inside of the middle loin bone. This fillet should not be confused with the best end of leg which, when boned, is sometimes referred to as a fillet. Tenderloin or fillet can be sliced, and grilled or fried, or flattened out for escalopes, coated in egg and breadcrumbs, and fried.

Shoulder

The shoulder is a large roasting joint, which is sometimes sold boned and rolled. Usually, though, it is divided into spare rib, blade bone, and hand and spring joints. All of these are economical cuts, which can be roasted on the bone or boned and stuffed. The spare rib joint is also sold cut into spare rib chops, which can be braised, grilled or fried.

Hand and spring

This is less expensive than the hind-quarter leg; in fact it is the cheapest part of the pig, other than the head, and it can be roasted whole on the bone. The hand and spring can be divided into the hand and shank. The hand can be used in many ways—cut up for pies, casseroles or stews, roasted with or without the bone, or boiled and served cold. The shank is usually boned out and used in pies, casseroles and soups. These cuts are usually what the butcher will sell as mince or pie pork.

Ham and Bacon

Pork in various forms and cuts can be cured or preserved to produce ham and bacon, both of which can be used as the centrepiece of a meal, or make delicious extras to a wide variety of other meals.

Ham

Ham consists of the complete leg of pork, which is cured separately. There is a variety of cutting processes that give different flavours, such as the York or Braddenham hams. Ham is often pre-cooked and served sliced.

Bacon

The complete carcase is divided into two sides: these, cured in a special brine, provide green bacon. This bacon can be further cured to produce smoked ham, ready for serving.

Ham and Bacon joints

Gammon hock is a perfect cured cut for boiling or

braising in water or cider. It can be served hot or cold. The hock can also be roasted.

Middle gammon can be cut into ½ inch (1¼cm) slices, grilled and served as gammon steaks, or it can be cooked whole and served as a complete joint.

Forehock can be boned and rolled: it is excellent boiled, braised or roasted. Collar is an ideal joint for boiling or roasting, and can be served hot or cold.

To cook ham or bacon joints
Soak the joint for several hours before cooking. If it is smoked it should be soaked overnight. Calculate the cooking time from the weight of the joint: allow 20 minutes per pound (500g), and 20 minutes over, for both boiling and roasting. A combination of the two gives excellent results: cover the joint with cold water (adding a carrot and an onion if you like), bring to the boil and simmer for half the total cooking time. Then drain and dry the meat, place it in a roasting tin in the oven, 350°F (180°C), Gas 4, for the remaining time. Remove the skin and coat with golden crumbs. Serve hot or cold.

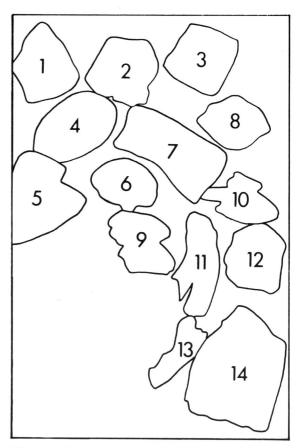

The cuts of pork:
1 *thick end of belly* **2** *hand and spring* **3** *prime middle of belly* **4** *fillet or best end of leg* **5** *knuckle end of leg* **6** *chump end of loin* **7** *rib end of loin* **8** *blade* **9** *loin chops* **10** *kidney pork chops* **11** *pork fillet or tenderloin* **12** *middle of loin* **13** *middle of loin* **14** *spare rib joint*

Carving Pork

Loin

To make carving easier first free the chine bone with a small sharp knife. Some people prefer to leave the crackling on and carve the joint along the score marks to make their slices. Alternatively, you can remove the crackling, carving it separately, and serve thinner slices for the individual portions. You can make the slices bigger by carving at a slight angle.

Hand of pork

Remove the crackling, slice and serve it with each helping. Now remove the rib bones from the underside. Then carve downward slices from each side of the bone. The joint is fattier on the underside, and you may want to remove some fat before serving each portion. Carve right down on both sides until you reach the bone; then detach each individual slice by carving next to the bone and across the grain.

Roast Pork

Choose a joint suitable for roasting, referring to the list of cuts above. For crunchy crackling, ask the butcher to score the skin, then brush with oil and sprinkle heavily with salt, rubbing it well into the cuts. If liked, stuff with sage and onion stuffing. Roast for longer than other meats—30 minutes per pound (500g), plus 30 minutes extra at 375°F (190°C), Gas 5. Accompany with roast and/or boiled potatoes, apple or cranberry sauce (see below), sage and onion stuffing (if liked), green vegetables and Bisto gravy.

In general, the amounts to allow per person are:

8 to 12oz (225 to 350g) pork with bone

or

4 to 6oz (125 to 175g) pork without bone

Freezing

Made-up dishes or pieces of cooked pork may be frozen for up to 6 months.

Apple sauce (serves 6 to 8)
1lb (500g) cooking apples
3 tbsp water
4 level tsp granulated sugar
1 rounded tsp butter
salt to taste

1 Peel and core apples. Put into pan with water. Bring to boil. Cover. Lower heat. Simmer gently till soft and puffy.
2 Beat to a light snow. Add sugar and butter. Continue to beat over low heat until sugar dissolves. Season. Serve cold.

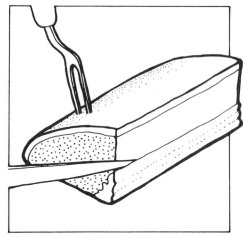

Carving loin of pork: free the chine bone

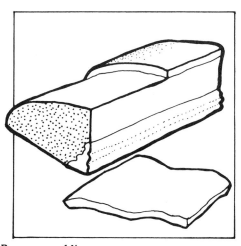

Remove crackling

Cut downward slices

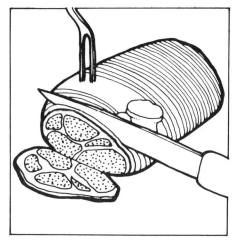

Carving hand of pork

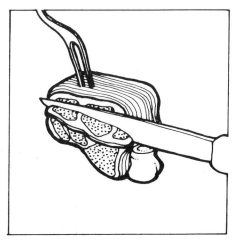

Cut right down to the bone on both sides

Cranberry sauce (serves 6 to 8)
¼pt (150ml) water
8oz (225g) fresh cranberries
6oz (175g) granulated sugar

1 Put water and cranberries into saucepan. Cook, uncovered, until skins split and fruit is soft; allow about 7 to 10 minutes.
2 Remove from heat. Add sugar. Stir until dissolved. Serve sauce cold.

Stuffed Pork Cabbage Leaves (serves 4)

An adaptation of Greek stuffed vine leaves.

8 large green cabbage leaves

Filling
½oz (15g) butter or margarine
1 small onion, peeled and chopped
2 small carrots, peeled and coarsely grated
2oz (50g) long-grain rice
2 level tsp Bisto
½pt (275ml) cold water
8oz (225g) cold cooked pork, finely chopped
1 level tsp salt
pepper to taste

Sauce
3 level tbsp tomato purée
½pt (275ml) boiling water

1 Put leaves into large pan. Cover with boiling water. Boil gently 5 minutes. Drain. Rinse under cold water.
2 Stand leaves on board and cut out hard pieces of stalk at base of each.
3 For filling, heat butter or margarine in pan. Add onion and carrots and fry 5 minutes, turning. Stir in rice.
4 Mix Bisto to a smooth paste with a little cold water. Blend in rest of water. Add to vegetable and rice mixture. Bring to boil. Cover. Simmer 10 minutes.
5 Stir in pork. Add seasoning. Mix well. Spoon equal amounts on to cabbage leaves. 'Parcel' each one up individually by folding sides of leaf over filling and rolling-up.
6 Transfer to shallow ovenproof dish with joins underneath. Mix tomato purée with boiling water. Pour over cabbage rolls.
7 Cover with lid or foil. Cook ¾ hour in oven set to 350°F (180°C), Gas 4.
   Serve with creamed potatoes.

Stuffed Pork Roll (serves 6 to 8)

An appetising dish for summer eating which is easy to make and economical.

2 level tbsp sage-and-onion stuffing mix
2 level tsp Bisto
4 tbsp boiling water
8oz (225g) beef sausagemeat
3lb (1½kg) piece pickled pork belly, boned
toasted breadcrumbs

1 Mix together stuffing, Bisto and boiling water. Add sausagemeat and knead in well with hands.
2 Place pork, skin side down, on work surface. Spoon stuffing along centre then bring meat round stuffing to form a roll. Tie at close intervals with fine string.
3 Stand in saucepan and cover with cold water. Bring to boil and skim. Lower heat.
4 Cover pan and simmer pork very gently for 3 hours. Remove from water and leave to cool. Foil-wrap when cold. Refrigerate overnight.
5 Open up foil and remove string. Cut away skin from pork then coat all over with crumbs, pressing them on with your finger tips.
   Slice and serve with salad.

Egg and Crumbed Pork Escalopes (serves 4)

An economical version of veal escalopes or the famous Wiener Schnitzel.

12oz (350g) fillet of pork
1 level tbsp flour
2 heaped tsp Onion Bisto
1 × Grade 2 (large) egg, beaten with 1 tbsp milk
4oz (125g) fresh white breadcrumbs
oil for frying

Garnish
freshly fried button mushrooms
sliced gherkins
lemon wedges

1 Cut pork fillet in half lengthwise. Place between two sheets of greaseproof paper and beat firmly with a rolling pin to flatten.
2 Using a sharp knife, divide each piece into 4 escalopes.
3 Coat evenly with flour, first mixed with Bisto. Dip in beaten-egg mixture then coat with crumbs.
4 Fry, 2 or 3 at a time, in hot oil for about 10 minutes, turning twice.
5 Drain on paper towels. Arrange on a warm platter as shown in the picture. Garnish with mushrooms, gherkins and lemon.
   Serve with sauté potatoes or chips.

Sweet lamb casserole

Toad-in-the-Hole (serves 4)

4oz (125g) plain flour
pinch salt
1 × Grade 2 (large) egg
¼pt (150ml) milk
¼pt (150ml) cold water
2oz (50g) lard, dripping or butter
8 large pork sausages

1 To make batter, sift flour and salt into bowl. Using a whisk, mix to a thick and creamy batter with egg and milk. Beat briskly for 10 minutes.
2 Gradually blend in cold water. When batter is smooth, pour into bowl and refrigerate, covered, for 1 hour.
3 Put fat into roasting tin. Heat till sizzling in oven set to 400°F (200°C), Gas 6. Add sausages. Bake 10 minutes.
4 Pour batter into tin over sausages. Bake 40 to 45 minutes, when batter should be well-risen, golden and crisp.
   Serve with ½pt (275ml) gravy made with Bisto Rich Gravy Granules, baked jacket potatoes and peas.

Bacon Batter Pudding (serves 4)

Make exactly as toad-in-the-hole, substituting 8 rashers of rolled-up bacon for the sausages. Serve with the same accompaniments.

Corned Beef Batter Pudding

Make exactly as toad-in-the-hole, substituting 12oz (350g) corned beef, cut into large dice, for the sausages. Serve with the same accompaniments.

Cottage Pie with Pork and Mushrooms (serves about 4)

½pt (275ml) gravy made with Bisto Rich Gravy Granules
4oz (125g) trimmed mushrooms, sliced with stalks
3oz (75g) butter or margarine
3oz (75g) onion, chopped
crumbs from 1 slice wholemeal bread
12oz (350g) cold cooked pork, minced
salt and pepper to taste
1lb (500g) freshly cooked potatoes
warm milk

1 Stand gravy over low heat. In separate pan, fry mushrooms briskly in 2oz (50g) butter or margarine for 3 minutes. Add onion. Fry until golden.
2 Add mushrooms and onions to gravy with breadcrumbs and pork, and salt and pepper to taste.
3 Transfer to buttered heatproof dish. Mash potatoes finely. Work in remaining butter or margarine. Beat to a light snow with milk.
4 Pile over pork mixture. Reheat ½ hour in oven set to 400°F (200°C), Gas 6.
  Serve with green vegetables.

Pork Sausage Fritters (serves 4)

Make batter exactly as given in recipe for Italian fritto misto on page 113. Gently boil 1lb (500g) pork sausages till cooked through, allowing about 10 to 15 minutes. Drain and cool. Coat with batter. Fry in deep hot fat till golden and crisp. Drain on paper towels. Serve with chips and salad.

Pork 'n' Cabbage (serves 4 to 6)

An economical dish, made with pork sausages and red cabbage. It has a slightly sweet-sour tang and originated in Eastern Europe.

2lb (1kg) red cabbage
2oz (50g) lard or white cooking fat
1lb (500g) Bramley apples
2 level tbsp golden syrup
½ level tsp caraway seeds
½pt (275ml) water
bouquet garni
3 heaped tsp Onion Bisto
3 tbsp malt vinegar
salt and pepper to taste
1lb (500g) pork chipolata sausages

1 Finely shred cabbage. Heat lard or fat in heavy pan. Add cabbage. Stir round till cabbage is lightly coated with fat. Cover pan. Cook *gently*, over minimal heat, for 5 minutes.

2 Meanwhile, peel and slice apples. Add to cabbage with syrup, caraway seeds, water and bouquet garni. Cover. Simmer 2 hours or until cabbage is very soft and mahogany-red. Stir frequently.
3 To thicken, mix Bisto smoothly with the vinegar. Stir into cabbage mixture. Cook slowly, stirring continuously, till thickened.
4 Adjust seasoning to taste, then serve piping hot with the pork sausages freshly grilled or fried, and boiled potatoes.

Party Pork Curry (serves about 12)

3 tbsp salad oil
1lb (500g) onions, chopped
4 garlic cloves, crushed
3½lb (1½kg) hand and spring of pork (boned weight)
2 level tsp Bisto
4 level tsp mild Madras curry powder
3 rounded tbsp tomato purée
1 level tbsp garam masala
½pt (275ml) hot water
1 level tsp salt
2 tbsp lemon juice
2 rounded tbsp orange marmalade
2 bay leaves
1 level tsp cumin seeds
12 whole cardamom
1oz (25g) creamed coconut

1 Heat oil in large and sturdy saucepan. Add onions and garlic. Fry gently, with lid on pan, until pale gold.
2 Cut meat into 1 inch (2½cm) cubes. Add to pan. Increase heat slightly. Fry briskly until well sealed and golden.
3 Stir in Bisto, curry powder, purée, garam masala, and hot water. Bring slowly to boil. Add all remaining ingredients except coconut.
4 Lower heat. Cover. Simmer gently about 1½ hours or until meat is tender, stirring frequently to prevent sticking.
5 Add creamed coconut, first broken up into small pieces. Stir until melted.
6 Transfer curry to a large serving dish.
  Accompany with Basmati rice and side dishes (sambals) of cut-up fresh pineapple, mango chutney, grated fresh coconut and lime pickle.

Curried lamb soup

Orange pork meatballs

Orange Pork Meatballs (serves 4)

12oz (350g) pork belly (middle cut), minced
1 medium dessert apple, peeled and grated
finely grated peel of 1 large orange
1 packet sage-and-onion stuffing mix
1 egg yolk, beaten
3 tbsp salad oil
1 can (11oz or 300g) mandarin oranges
water
4 rounded tsp Bisto
2 rounded tbsp orange marmalade

1 Mix the minced pork with the apple and half the orange rind.
2 Make up the stuffing mix according to packet directions and work into the pork. Add the beaten yolk.
3 Form into 8 meatballs, using floured hands if the mixture is sticky. Chill for ½ hour.
4 Fry the meatballs gently in oil until browned all over. Put into a casserole.
5 Drain the mandarin oranges and make up the juice to 1pt (575ml) with water.
6 Blend the Bisto to a smooth paste with a little of the juice and water, then add remainder.
7 Stir in the marmalade and pour the Bisto liquid over the meatballs.
8 Cover the casserole and cook for ¾ hour at 350°F (180°C), Gas 4.
9 Add the drained mandarin oranges and cook for a further 15 minutes. Garnish with remaining grated orange rind.
   Serve with chips and a large green salad.

Pot-roasted Pork with Vegetables (serves 6 to 8)

1oz (25g) lard or margarine
12oz (350g) carrots, thinly sliced
8oz (225g) onions, thinly sliced
4 medium celery stalks, sliced
2 level tsp Bisto
water
salt and pepper to taste
4 to 4½ (2 to 2¼kg) hand of pork
2oz (50g) elbow or short macaroni

1 Heat lard or margarine in large pan. Add vegetables. Fry gently 5 minutes.
2 In measuring cup, mix Bisto smoothly with a little water. Make up to ¾pt (425ml) with extra water.
3 Add to vegetables in pan. Bring to boil, stirring. Season to taste. Add pork. Cover. Simmer 2 hours, or longer if necessary, until meat is tender.
4 Lift pork out of pan. Remove skin and knuckle. Place meat on warm serving dish. Keep hot.
5 Add macaroni to vegetables and gravy in pan. Boil 10 minutes. Adjust seasoning. Ladle contents of pan round pork. Cut meat into slices.

Pork and Prune Casserole (serves 4 to 6)

8oz (225g) pack of dried prunes, soaked overnight in cold tea
2lb (1kg) pork spare-rib chops
2 tbsp salad oil
1 rounded tbsp flour
3 rounded tsp Onion Bisto
½pt (275ml) water
¼pt (150ml) apple juice
salt and pepper to taste

1 Drain prunes, and remove stones.

2 Remove excess fat from pork. Fry in oil until browned. Place in casserole. Add prunes.

3 Mix flour and Bisto smoothly with a little of the cold water. Blend in remaining water and apple juice. Season and pour over pork and prunes.

4 Cover and cook 1 hour at 375°F (190°C), Gas 5. Serve with creamed potatoes and green vegetables.

Pork and Vegetable Hotpot with Apples (serves 4 to 6)

1½lb (750g) unsalted pork belly
1 level tbsp flour mixed with 3 heaped tsp Bisto
1oz (25g) margarine or dripping
1 or 2 tsp salad oil
8oz (225g) onions, chopped
1pt (575ml) water
4 medium carrots, each cut lengthwise into strips
8 medium potatoes, peeled but left whole
2 medium celery stalks, thinly sliced
1 small turnip, diced
2 heaped tbsp finely chopped parsley
2 large dessert apples
2oz (50g) stoned prunes, soaked overnight in a little gin

1 Cube meat. Toss in flour and Bisto mixture. Heat margarine or dripping in large pan. Add pork. Fry till golden brown and crisp. Remove to plate temporarily.

2 Add onions to remaining fat in pan, adding oil at the same time. Fry gently until pale gold. Replace pork cubes. Mix well.

3 Transfer to casserole. Add water, carrots, potatoes, celery, turnip and parsley. Cover. Cook 2 hours in oven set to 350°F (180°C), Gas 4.

4 Peel, core and slice apples. Add to casserole with prunes and any left-over gin. Cover. Continue to cook another ½ hour.

Serve hot with green vegetables.

Note

To remove surplus fat, leave hotpot overnight in the cool. Remove layer of fat. Reheat in saucepan.

Pork Stew with Apricots and Raisins (serves 4 to 6)

1½lb (750g) hand of pork, cubed
1 level tbsp flour mixed with 3 heaped tsp Onion Bisto
2oz (50g) dripping
2 medium garlic cloves, crushed
8oz (225g) cooking apricots, stoned and sliced
½pt (275ml) water
1oz (25g) raisins
salt and pepper to taste

1 Coat meat cubes in flour and Bisto mixture. Fry in the dripping until well-sealed and brown.

2 Add garlic, apricots, water and raisins. Cook, stirring, until mixture comes to boil and thickens. Season.

3 Lower heat. Cover. Simmer about 1½ hours or until pork is tender, stirring occasionally.

Serve with baked jacket potatoes and green vegetables to taste.

Prune and pork casserole

Boston Baked Beans (serves about 8)

An authentic recipe which is marvellous to make in a slow cooker or in an Aga-type slow oven.

1lb (500g) small white haricot beans
8oz (225g) salted pork belly
4 level tsp powder mustard
4oz (125g) soft brown sugar (dark variety)
2oz (50g) black treacle
2oz (50g) golden syrup
2 level tbsp tomato purée
2 level tsp salt
1 medium peeled onion, studded with 2 cloves
2 level tbsp bacon dripping

1 Wash beans. Soak overnight in enough water to cover. Do not drain. Tip into a heavy-based pan.
2 Bring slowly to boil. Lower heat. Cover. Simmer for 1 hour or until beans are tender; they may take up to ½ hour longer, depending on the bean.
3 Cut a slice off the piece of salt pork and place in bottom of a deepish casserole. Drain beans, reserving liquid. Put beans into casserole on top of pork.
4 Blend next 6 ingredients with reserved bean water. Pour over beans. Bury onion somewhere in the middle.
5 Cut gashes in the remaining piece of salt pork. Stand on top of beans. Cover and cook about 6 to 8 hours in oven set to 300°F (150°C), Gas 2.
6 Check liquid level periodically and top up with a little boiling water when necessary.
7 Uncover casserole for last hour of cooking to crisp the pork. Add bacon dripping at this stage and stir in well. Adjust seasoning to taste.

Sweet and Sour Pork (serves 4 to 6)

1½lb (750g) pie pork
1oz (25g) butter or margarine
1 level tbsp flour
3 slightly rounded tsp Onion Bisto
1 can (8oz or 225g) pineapple slices
1 small green pepper, de-seeded and sliced
2 level tbsp soft brown sugar
2 tsp tomato ketchup
2 tsp Worcestershire sauce
2 tbsp vinegar
1 level tbsp mango chutney or sweet pickle
salt
8oz (225g) long-grain rice, freshly cooked

1 Cut meat into 1 inch (2½cm) cubes. Heat butter or margarine in pan. Add pork cubes. Fry 5 minutes. Stir in flour and Bisto. Leave over low heat.
2 Pour pineapple syrup into pan and make up to ½pt (275ml) with water. Add to pan with pepper, sugar, ketchup, Worcestershire sauce, vinegar, chutney or pickle, and salt.

3 Cut up 2 pineapple rings and add to pan, stirring in well. Reserve rest of rings. Bring pork mixture slowly to boil, stirring. Lower heat and cover.
4 Simmer about ¾ to 1 hour or until meat is tender.
Arrange on a warm dish then surround with a border of rice. Garnish with rest of pineapple rings, cut up into small pieces.

Dutch Indonesian Hash (serves 6)

2oz (50g) margarine
8oz (225g) onions, finely chopped
1 rounded tbsp flour
3 rounded tsp Bisto
¾pt (425ml) water
bouquet garni
1lb (500g) cold cooked pork, diced
4 tbsp vinegar
1 tbsp soy sauce
salt and pepper to taste

1 Heat margarine in heavy pan. Add onions. Fry gently till light gold.
2 Stir in flour and Bisto. Gradually blend in water. Heat till thickened and bubbly.
3 Add bouquet garni, pork, vinegar, soy sauce and salt and pepper to taste. Cover. Simmer gently 20 minutes, stirring periodically.
Serve hot with boiled potatoes.

Lamb moussaka

Moroccan chick pea and lamb stew

Piquant Belgian Pork (serves 4)

1oz (25g) lard or butter
4 pieces pork fillet, *each* 4 to 6oz (125 to 175g)
3oz (75g) onion
1 level tbsp flour
3 heaped tsp Bisto
¾pt (425ml) tomato juice
2 tsp malt vinegar
1 level tsp caster sugar
3 level tbsp chopped gherkins
½ level tsp tarragon
1 level tsp Dijon mustard
salt and pepper to taste

1 Heat lard or butter in heavy pan. Add pork. Fry briskly until golden brown on both sides. Remove to plate temporarily.
2 Add onion to remaining fat in pan. Fry until pale gold. Stir in flour and Bisto. Blend in tomato juice and vinegar. Bring to boil, stirring.
3 Add rest of ingredients. Replace pork. Cover. Simmer ¾ to 1 hour or until pork is tender and cooked through.
 Accompany with boiled potatoes.

Pork Goulash (serves 4 to 6)

1oz (25g) flour
6 rounded tsp Bisto
2 level tbsp paprika (mild red pepper)
3lb (1½kg) blade of pork, boned and cubed
2oz (50g) butter or margarine
1 large onion, sliced
1 can (14oz or 400g) tomatoes
½pt (275ml) water
1 rounded tsp caster sugar
salt and pepper to taste
1 carton (5oz or 142ml) soured cream

1 Mix the flour, Bisto and paprika in a bowl. Add the cubed meat and toss to coat.
2 Melt the butter or margarine in a large pan. Add the onion and fry for 5 minutes.
3 Add the coated meat to the pan and fry quickly to brown and seal.
4 Stir in the tomatoes, water and sugar. Bring to the boil and either simmer, covered, in the saucepan for 1½ hours, or cook for 2 hours at 350°F (180°C), Gas 4, in a covered casserole.
5 Spoon soured cream over the goulash.
 Serve with boiled rice or egg noodles.

Chinese Pork Spare Ribs (serves 4)

These are meaty pork bones which are traditionally part of a good Chinese meal. To make them at home, give your butcher (or even local supermarket) some advance warning.

12 to 16 spare-rib pork bones, separated
3 tbsp clear honey or golden syrup
1 tbsp soy sauce
2 level tsp Onion Bisto
1 medium garlic clove, crushed
¼ level tsp ground cinnamon
½ level tsp ground ginger
1 tbsp lemon juice
2 tbsp dry white wine, dry sherry or apple juice

1 Place spare rib bones in large roasting tin. Cook ¾ hour in oven set to 350°F (180°C), Gas 4.
2 Pour away fat and discard. Place rest of ingredients into saucepan. Warm gently together. Brush over spare ribs.
3 Return to oven and cook a further 30 to 40 minutes or until bones are golden brown and glazed-looking.
4 Turn twice during cooking and brush with any left-over honey mixture.
 Serve with stir-fry rice (recipe below).

Stir-fry rice
1 tbsp salad oil
4oz (100 to 125g) onion, finely chopped
8oz (225g) cooked rice (cooked weight)
½ small can (8oz or 225g) bamboo shoots, drained
1oz (25g) flaked almonds, lightly toasted
1 small can (7½oz or 212g) small mushrooms in
 brine, drained
2 tsp soy sauce
salt and pepper to taste
2 × Grade 2 (large) eggs, thoroughly beaten

1 Heat oil in heavy-based pan. Add onion. Fry until light gold. Keep pan covered and allow about 7 to 10 minutes.
2 Stir in rice and bamboo shoots. Heat through, fork-stirring non-stop, until very hot.
3 Add all remaining ingredients. Cook, fork-stirring still, until eggs are lightly scrambled.
 Serve straight away with pork.

Danish Pork Liver Pâté (serves about 8)

An especially appetising and rich pâté that makes a splendid first course for any occasion.

7oz (200g) unsalted pork belly with rind removed
12oz (350g) pork liver
6oz (175g) onions
2 tsp anchovy essence or 1oz (25g) canned anchovies
 in oil
1oz (25g) plain flour
3 rounded tsp Bisto
¼pt (150ml) milk
4 tbsp double cream
1 × Grade 3 (standard) egg
½ level tsp ground nutmeg or mace
salt and freshly milled black pepper to taste

Danish pork liver pate

1 Dice pork belly and liver. Cut onions into eighths. Mince the 3 ingredients finely together, adding anchovy essence or anchovies.

2 Gradually beat in rest of ingredients. Transfer to a 2lb (1kg) loaf tin with base and sides lined with greased foil.

3 Spread evenly with a knife. Cover with more greased foil. Stand in small roasting tin. Add sufficient cold water to reach about 2 inches (5cm) up the sides of the tin containing the pâté.

4 Cook 1¾ hours in oven set to 350°F (180°C), Gas 4. Remove from oven. Leave to stand ¼ hour. Pour off fat carefully. Cover with clean foil.

5 Leave till lukewarm. Unmould and take off foil. Chill several hours before slicing.

Accompany with hot toast.

Note
The mixture is very soft before cooking but firms up later.

Indonesian Saté Sticks (serves 4)

1lb (500g) pork fillet
3oz (75g) onion
1 large garlic clove
3 level tsp ground coriander
2 level tsp Bisto
2 level tsp Sambal Manis (available from oriental grocers and other speciality shops)
1 tbsp soy sauce
1 level tbsp soft brown sugar
salt and pepper to taste

1 Cut meat into ½ inch (1¼cm) cubes. Place in earthenware or enamel dish.

2 To make marinade, cut up onion and blend in blender goblet to thickish purée with next 6 ingredients. Season to taste.

3 Pour over pork cubes. Toss well to mix. Cover. Refrigerate 5 to 6 hours.

4 Before serving, thread cubes onto 8 skewers (bamboo ones for preference). Grill until cooked through (about 8 to 10 minutes) turning twice.

Accompany with freshly cooked rice, prawn crackers (available in packs) and the piquant peanut sauce which follows.

Piquant peanut sauce
3oz (75g) onion
1 medium garlic clove
2 tsp salad or groundnut oil
6oz (175g) smooth peanut butter
1 level tsp soft brown sugar
1 tbsp lemon juice
½pt (275ml) boiling water
1 level tsp Sambal Manis (optional)
salt and pepper to taste

1 Finely chop onion. Crush garlic. Fry both in the oil until pale gold. Stir in peanut butter and sugar.

2 Gradually blend in lemon juice and water. Cook, stirring, until sauce comes to boil and is perfectly smooth.

3 Stir in Sambal Manis (if used) and season to taste. Serve as a dip for the saté sticks.

Portuguese Pork (serves 6)

2lb (1kg) hand of pork (boned weight) cubed
¼pt (150ml) rosé wine
4 tbsp mild vinegar
2 large garlic cloves, crushed
1 large bay leaf, crumbled
1 level tsp mixed herbs
½ level tsp salt
6 tsp salad oil
3 level tsp Onion Bisto

1 Place pork in enamel or earthenware dish with next 6 ingredients. Stir well to mix. Cover. Refrigerate about 12 hours, tossing cubes in the marinade twice or three times.
2 Remove pork from marinade. Fry in hot oil until golden brown. Stir in Bisto. Gradually add strained marinade.
3 Bring gently to boil, stirring. Lower heat. Cover pan. Simmer pork gently till tender, allowing about 1 hour.
   Serve with boiled potatoes and salad.

Romanian-style Baked Pork Chops (serves 4)

4 pork chops, each minimum of 6oz (175g)
4 level tsp Bisto
1lb (500g) potatoes, sliced
freshly milled black pepper
4oz (125g) Hungarian salami, chopped
4oz (125g) unsmoked gammon, chopped
2oz (50g) lard or white cooking fat
4oz (125g) onion, finely chopped
2 level tsp paprika
¼pt (150ml) water

1 Sprinkle both sides of chops with Bisto. Stand in oblong casserole so that they form a single layer over base.
2 Cover with potato slices. Sprinkle with pepper, salami and gammon. Leave on one side temporarily.
3 Heat lard or fat in frying pan. Add onion. Fry very gently until pale gold. Stir in paprika and water.
4 Heat till bubbling. Pour gently over chops in casserole.
5 Cover with lid or foil. Cook 1 hour in oven set to 350°F (180°C), Gas 4, uncovering for last 20 minutes or so to brown the chops.
6 Serve chops, with juices from casserole, with a selection of mixed vegetables or hot sauerkraut.

Pork Chop Espagnole (serves 4)

Make sauce as for Grilled Chicken Espagnole on page 92 but replace chicken with pork chops. Choose 4 chops—each weighing about 4oz (125g)—and grill about 10 to 12 minutes, brushing lightly with oil or melted butter. Turn at least twice.

Pork Chops Neapolitan (serves 4)

Follow recipe for Bacon Chops Neapolitan on page 78 but substitute pork chops (each 4oz or 125g) for bacon chops. Cook in oven ¼ hour longer and, for a non-greasy result, cut away excess fat from chops.

Pork Chops Pizzaiola

Make as Steak Pizzaiola (page 29), substituting pork chops for steak. Grill or fry the chops, making sure they are well cooked through.

Italian Pork Roast (serves 6)

3lb (1½kg) loin of pork (skin scored)
2 garlic cloves
fresh sage leaves or dried sage
¼pt (150ml) Chianti
salt
1 bay leaf
4 heaped tsp Bisto

1 Stand pork in roasting tin, scored side uppermost.
2 Cut garlic into thin strips. Make slits in pork flesh. Insert strips of garlic and pieces of sage leaves (or sprinkling of dried sage) into each slit.
3 Pour Chianti into tin over joint. Sprinkle heavily with salt for crisp skin. Add bay leaf.
4 Roast 2½ hours in oven set to 350°F (180°C), Gas 4, basting once only.
5 Remove pork to board. Measure juices from tin and make up to ½pt (275ml) with water if necessary.
6 Combine with Bisto to make a gravy as directed on the packet. Carve the joint.
   Serve with spinach, sauté potatoes and the gravy.

Bacon in Prune and Cider Sauce

1oz (25g) butter
2oz (50g) onion
4 rounded tsp Bisto
2 rounded tsp cornflour
½pt (275ml) dry cider
1 level tbsp tomato ketchup
1 level tsp mild German or French mustard
12oz (350g) cooked gammon, cubed
4oz (125g) stoned prunes, soaked overnight
salt and pepper to taste
¼pt (150g) single cream

1 Heat butter in pan. Add onion. Fry gently until pale gold. Stir in Bisto and cornflour.
2 Gradually blend in cider. Cook, stirring, until sauce comes to the boil and thickens.
3 Whisk in ketchup and mustard. Add gammon and prunes. Season to taste.
4 Simmer gently for 20 minutes. Whisk in cream. Reheat.
   Serve with macaroni and green vegetables to taste.

Stuffed pork cabbage leaves

Bacon with Cumberland sauce

Bacon with Cumberland Sauce (serves 8)

Another excellent dish for entertaining, with a fine old English sauce.

4lb (2kg) bacon forehock
water
1 medium onion, peeled but left whole
1 medium celery stalk
1 bay leaf
1 small parsley sprig
soft brown sugar

Sauce
1 level tsp prepared English mustard
2 tbsp soft brown sugar (dark)
¼ level tsp powdered ginger
3 drops Tabasco
½pt (275ml) dry red wine or port
4 cloves
4 rounded tsp Bisto
2 tbsp cold water
4 tbsp redcurrant jelly
1 level tsp *each* finely grated lemon and orange peel
juice of 1 small lemon and orange
salt and pepper to taste

1 Put bacon into large pan. Cover with water. Bring to boil. Drain. Cover with fresh water. Add onion, broken-up celery stalk, bay leaf and parsley.
2 Bring to boil. Skim. Lower heat. Cover. Simmer gently 2¼ hours. Lift out of water. Strip off skin. Cover fat with sugar. Glaze by transferring bacon to tin and cooking for about ¼ hour in oven set to 425°F (220°C), Gas 7.
3 To make sauce, put the mustard, sugar, ginger and Tabasco into pan. Mix smoothly with a little wine. Add rest of wine (or port).

4 Add cloves. Bring mixture slowly to the boil. Mix Bisto smoothly with cold water. Add to pan with rest of ingredients.
5 Bring to a gentle bubble, stirring continuously. Simmer 15 minutes.

To serve, carve hot bacon into slices and pass the sauce separately. Accompany with boiled potatoes and green vegetables to taste.

Gammon Steaks with Cumberland Sauce (serves 8)

Grill 8 gammon steaks to taste. Serve with Cumberland sauce prepared as directed in above recipe. Garnish with watercress.

Accompany with creamed or sauté potatoes and vegetables to taste.

Bacon with Raisin Brandy Sauce (serves 8)

Cook 4lb (2kg) bacon forehock or a piece of gammon as directed in recipe for bacon with Cumberland sauce. Coat with sugar and glaze in the oven as directed.

Serve with the sauce given below.

Raisin sauce
2oz (50g) seedless raisins
½pt (275ml) sweet white wine
3 cloves
½ level tsp finely grated orange peel
2 level tsp Bisto
1 level tsp cornflour
2oz (50g) soft brown sugar
2 tbsp fresh orange juice
½oz (15g) butter
1 tbsp brandy

1 Put the raisins, wine, cloves and orange peel into saucepan. Bring slowly to boil. Lower heat. Cover. Simmer ¼ hour.

2 Mix Bisto, cornflour and sugar smoothly with orange juice. Pour into pan with butter. Boil, stirring, till thickened. Stir in brandy.

Fruited Gammon Rolls in Cider (serves 6)

3oz (75g) onion
1 medium cooking apple, peeled
4 canned peach halves, drained
1oz (25g) sultanas
2oz (50g) butter
4 tbsp water
3oz (75g) fresh white breadcrumbs
½ level tsp sage
2 level tsp Bisto
6 large gammon rashers (but not too thick), de-rinded
¼pt (150ml) dry cider
2 garlic cloves, crushed

1 Chop onion, apple and peach halves. Mix together. Stir in sultanas.

2 Heat butter in flameproof casserole. Add onion and fruit mixture. Fry, with lid on pan, for about 10 minutes or until soft.

3 Add water. Cook gently for 10 minutes. Stir in crumbs, sage and Bisto. Mix well. Leave to cool.

4 Spread each gammon rasher with equal amounts of stuffing. Roll up. Hold in place by spearing with wooden cocktail sticks.

5 Return to casserole. Coat with cider. Add garlic. Cover. Cook ¾ hour in oven set to 375°F (190°C), Gas 5.

Serve with creamed potatoes and a green vegetable.

Bacon Chops Creole (serves 6)

2 tbsp salad oil
1 large onion, fairly finely chopped
1 de-seeded green pepper, fairly finely chopped
1 large celery stalk, thinly sliced
1 level tsp flour
2 heaped tsp Bisto
1 level tsp brown sugar
large pinch cayenne pepper
1 garlic clove, crushed
2 tsp mild malt vinegar
1oz (25g) stoned green olives, finely chopped
1 can (about 1lb or 500g) tomatoes
salt and pepper to taste
6 prime back bacon chops

1 To make sauce, heat oil in heavy-based pan. Add onion, green pepper and celery. Fry gently until pale gold. Stir in flour and Bisto. Cook gently 2 to 3 minutes.

2 Stir in all remaining ingredients except bacon. Bring to boil, stirring constantly. Lower heat. Cover. Simmer ¾ hour.

3 About 10 minutes before sauce is ready, fry or grill bacon chops to taste, allowing 5 minutes per side. Transfer to 6 warm dinner plates and coat with sauce.

Accompany with freshly boiled rice.

Bacon and Egg Casserole (serves 4)

2 medium onions, sliced
1 large garlic clove, crushed
4 tbsp salad oil
4oz (100 to 125g) bacon pieces
2 level tsp Bisto
1 medium green pepper, de-seeded and cut into strips
1 medium aubergine, unpeeled and cubed
1 can (14oz or 400g) tomatoes
salt and pepper to taste
4 × Grade 3 (standard) eggs

1 Fry the onion and garlic gently in oil for 5 minutes.

2 Add the bacon pieces and cook for a further 5 minutes.

3 Add the Bisto, pepper, aubergine, canned tomatoes and salt and pepper.

4 Put into a shallow casserole. Cover and cook for ¾ hour at 350°F (180°C), Gas 4.

5 Make 4 hollows in the top of the vegetable mixture and carefully crack an egg into each.

6 Re-cover the casserole and return to the oven for a further 15 minutes.

Casseroled Bacon Pudding (serves 4 to 6)

1 pkt sage-and-onion stuffing mix
1 medium onion, chopped
2 tbsp oil
4oz (100 to 125g) bacon pieces
12oz (350g) sausage meat
3oz (75g) trimmed mushrooms, chopped
1 × Grade 3 (standard) egg, beaten
salt and pepper to taste
4 rounded tsp Bisto
¾pt (425ml) water

1 Make up the stuffing mix according to packet directions.
2 Fry the onion in the oil with the chopped bacon pieces for 4 minutes.
3 Mix the onion and bacon into the stuffing together with the sausage meat and mushrooms. Bind with beaten egg and add seasoning.
4 Press into a greased pudding basin and chill for 1 hour.
5 Unmould the pudding into a shallow casserole.
6 Blend Bisto to a smooth paste with a little of the water. Blend in rest of water. Pour around the pudding.
7 Cook 1 hour in oven set to 375°F (190°C), Gas 5. Spoon Bisto over pudding from time to time.

Cut into wedges and serve with coleslaw salad and baked jacket potatoes.

Bacon Chops Neapolitan (serves 4)

1½lb (750g) skinned tomatoes, chopped
3 tbsp salad oil
1 large celery stalk, very thinly sliced
3 large garlic cloves, crushed
1 level tsp caster sugar
¼pt (150ml) water
3 rounded tsp Onion Bisto
salt and pepper to taste
1 level tsp mixed herbs
2 level tbsp finely chopped parsley
4 bacon chops
1 level tbsp flour mixed with 2 level tsp Onion Bisto
grated Parmesan cheese for serving

1 Put tomatoes, 2 tbsp oil, celery, garlic, sugar, water and Bisto into pan.
2 Add salt and pepper to taste, the herbs and parsley. Bring to boil, stirring. Lower heat. Bubble, uncovered, for about ¾ hour until sauce is thick and purée-like.
3 Stir frequently to prevent sticking and keep heat under pan fairly low.
4 Coat chops with flour mixture, then fry in 1 tbsp oil until golden brown on both sides.
5 Spoon sauce over base of fairly shallow heatproof casserole. Arrange chops on top and sprinkle with salt and pepper.
6 Cover. Cook ½ hour in oven set to 350°F (180°C), Gas 4.

Serve with rice or pasta and green vegetables. Pass cheese separately.

Glazed Gammon with Cherries (serves 8 to 10)

4lb (2¼kg) middle of corner gammon, boned
water

Glaze
4oz (100 to 125g) soft brown sugar (dark variety)
1 level tsp powder mustard
1 level tsp ground ginger
1 level tsp Onion Bisto
4 tbsp orange juice

Decoration
halved glacé cherries
cloves

1 Cook gammon in water, allowing 30 minutes per pound (500g) and 30 minutes over (2½ hours in total).
2 Drain. Strip off skin and score fat into a diamond pattern with a sharp knife. Stand joint in roasting tin.
3 For glaze, mix sugar with mustard, ginger, Bisto and 2 tbsp of the orange juice.
4 Spread over gammon fat and pour rest of orange juice into tin.
5 Cook about ½ hour in oven set to 400°F (200°C), Gas 6, when fat should be crisp and golden-looking.
6 Stud with halved cherries and cloves.

Serve hot with vegetables and Bisto gravy, or cold with salad.

Note
To reduce saltiness, boil up gammon 2 or 3 times in fresh changes of cold water before cooking as above.

Glazed gammon with cherries

Main-meal Swedish Pea and Bacon Soup (serves 4)

1kg (2lb) unsmoked knuckle of bacon
water
½lb (225g) yellow split peas, soaked overnight then
  drained
1 medium leek, trimmed and slit, well washed and
  sliced
4oz (100 to 125g) carrots, sliced
6oz (175g) onions, chopped
2pt (about 1¼ litres) water
2 level tsp Bisto
½ level tsp marjoram
½ level tsp powdered ginger
seasoning to taste

1 Put bacon into large pan. Add water to cover. Boil
up. Drain.
2 Add peas, fresh vegetables and water to bacon
knuckle in pan. Bring to boil. Lower heat. Cover.
Simmer about 2 hours or until peas are soft and soup
is fairly thick. Stir frequently to prevent sticking.
3 Remove bacon from soup and cut flesh into small
pieces, discarding skin and bones. Return to soup
with rest of ingredients.
4 Reheat, stirring. Ladle into soup bowls.
  Serve very hot with brown bread.

4 Veal and Veal Dishes

Veal is a young and immature meat which should be used as soon as possible after purchase (unless frozen or bought fresh for freezer storage) to prevent deterioration and spoilage.

When choosing veal, make sure that the flesh is delicate pink in colour if buying very young meat; a deeper pink if the veal is older (something on which your butcher should advise you). Do not buy any veal if the flesh is flabby and beginning to turn brown. Fresh veal is easy to recognise because of white areas of connective tissue (which jellify when cooked) on the flesh, which are puffy and blistery in appearance. Also the fat is firm and white, and not soft and oily-looking.

Very young veal is less digestible than older veal, but both require thorough chewing and lively cooking methods to eliminate what some would describe as an insipid meat with an uninteresting taste. To ensure that veal is tender and easy to digest, it should be thoroughly cooked and never served under-done.

Cuts of Veal

Fillet (thick flank)
Fillet, from which escalopes or cutlets are cut, is the most esteemed and expensive cut of veal. It is taken from the top of the leg and is tender and delicately-flavoured. Fillet of veal can be roasted in the piece but it is more usual, in view of cost, to buy thin slices and have them beaten flat for escalopes.

Loin
A little cheaper than fillet but also expensive. The best end, with kidney, is considered a prime roasting joint. Chops are taken from this cut and the chump end is sometimes braised.

Shoulder
A cut which can be braised or roasted. As with lamb, the shoulder is often boned and stuffed before roasting.

Breast
An excellent stewing or braising cut. When boned and rolled, breast can be roasted satisfactorily.

Knuckle and neck (shin)
Suitable for long, slow methods of cooking such as stewing.

Calves' feet
When available, used for making jelly.

Rump
See Beef.

Silverside
See Beef.

Topside
See Beef.

Carving Veal
Both shoulder and breast of veal are usually boned before purchase and tied into shape, so they are easy to carve, with or without stuffing.

Loin on the bone can be carved in the same way as loin of pork—see page 00.

Roast Veal
Where veal is available and not too expensive, some people might like to serve roast veal for the weekend joint and the most suitable cuts are fillet, boned-out shoulder, loin and boned breast which is best rolled and tied.

Roast as pork—allow 30 minutes per pound (500g) plus 30 minutes extra, at 375°F (190°C), Gas 5. Traditional accompaniments are roast and/or boiled potatoes, assorted vegetables, bacon rolls and Bisto gravy.

Note
As veal is a dryish meat, it is advisable to roast it in a tin containing about 3oz (75g) butter, margarine or dripping. It should also be basted every ¼ hour.

Freezing
Made-up dishes or portions of cooked veal can be frozen for up to 6 months.

Roast Veal Piquant (serves 8)

Roast 3lb (1½kg) boned shoulder of veal as directed in recipe for roast veal on page 82. Serve with piquant sauce made as follows:

Make up 1pt (575ml) gravy, as directed on tin, using Bisto Rich Gravy Granules and boiling water. Stir in 2 level tsp drained and chopped capers, 1 level tbsp chopped gherkins, 2 tsp Worcestershire sauce, 1 tbsp mild malt vinegar and 1 tsp Dijon mustard. Stir well. Reheat.

Roast and Stuffed Veal Breast (serves 6 to 8)

3lb (1½kg) breast of veal, weighed after boning
salt and pepper
1 packed parsley and thyme stuffing mix
1 level tsp finely grated lemon peel
1 small onion, grated
1oz (25g) melted butter or melted dripping
8 rashers streaky bacon

1 Lay out veal on work surface. Sprinkle with salt and pepper to taste.
2 Tip stuffing mix into bowl. Add lemon peel and onion. Make up with water as directed on the packet.
3 Spread over veal to within 1 inch (2½cm) of edges. Roll up and tie securely at intervals with thin string or thick thread.
4 Stand in roasting tin. Brush with butter or dripping. Cover with bacon.
5 Roast for 2½ hours in oven preheated to 350°F (180°C), Gas 4, removing bacon rashers during the last ½ hour so that the joint can crispen.
6 Carve into fairly thick slices.
   Serve with gravy made with Bisto Rich Gravy Granules, the bacon, boiled potatoes tossed in butter, green beans and mushrooms.

Tangy Breast of Veal (serves 6)

4oz (100g) fresh white breadcrumbs
6oz (150g) sultanas
2oz (50g) suet
salt and black pepper
grated rind and juice of 1 orange
1 egg yolk, lightly beaten
approx 4½lb (2kg) breast of veal, boned
2oz (50g) lard

1 Prepare the stuffing; mix together the breadcrumbs, sultanas, suet, seasoning and grated orange rind. Add the egg yolk and enough orange juice to bind the mixture.
2 Spread the stuffing over the boned veal. Roll up and tie with thin string at 1 inch (2½cm) intervals.
3 Place the meat in a roasting tin, add the lard and roast for 2½ hours in the centre of the oven at 400°F (200°C), Gas 6, basting occasionally. Cover the meat with foil if it browns too quickly.

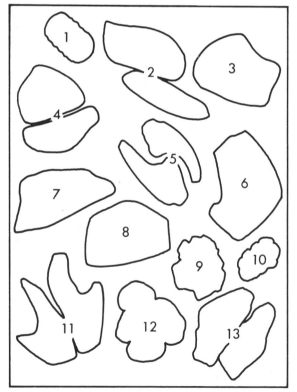

The cuts of veal:
1 *rolled shoulder* **2** *topside* **3** *breast* **4** *thick flank* **5**
loin chops **6** *loin* **7** *rump* **8** *silverside* **9, 10** *pie veal* **11**
best end of neck **12** *shin (Osso Bucco cut)* **13** *neck*

Creamy paprika veal

Creamy Paprika Veal (serves 6)

Passed on to me by a high-ranking chef working in Budapest, this is a fine dish with a delicate colour and subtle flavour. The Hungarians would use lard for frying but I find that is a little greasy.

1½lb (750g) stewing veal
1oz (25g) butter
2 tbsp salad oil
8oz (225g) onions, chopped
4oz (100 to 125g) unsmoked bacon, coarsely chopped
2 level tbsp paprika (bright orangy-red and mild)
2 large green peppers, de-seeded and cut into strips
8oz (225g) skinned tomatoes, de-seeded and flesh chopped
¼pt (150ml) plus 5 tbsp water
1oz (25g) cornflour
2 level tsp Bisto
½pt (275ml) whipping cream
2 tbsp lemon juice

1 Cut veal into strips. Heat butter and oil in large pan. Add veal. Fry fairly briskly until pale gold. Remove to plate.
2 Add onions and bacon to butter and oil in pan. Fry gently, with lid on pan, until soft but still pale. Allow ¼ hour.
3 Stir in paprika, green pepper, tomatoes and ¼pt (150ml) of the water. Stir well to mix. Replace veal. Slowly bring to boil, stirring. Lower heat. Cover. Simmer gently about 1 hour or until meat is tender.
4 To thicken, mix cornflour and Bisto to a smooth liquid with the 5 tbsp water. Add to veal. Stir until thickened and bubbly.
5 Mix cream and lemon juice well together. Stir into veal mixture and remove from heat. Spoon on to warm plates.

Serve with freshly cooked pasta shells. A green salad, tossed with a mild French dressing, also makes an excellent accompaniment.

Brandied Veal (serves 6)

2lb (1kg) pie veal, already cubed by the butcher
2 level tbsp flour mixed with 3 heaped tsp Bisto
1oz (25g) butter
3 tsp salad oil
8oz (225g) onion, chopped
1 large garlic clove, crushed
2 heaped tbsp tomato purée
½pt (275ml) dry white wine
8oz (225g) tomatoes, skinned and chopped
1 level tsp salt
bouquet garni
4oz (100 to 125g) mushrooms and stalks, trimmed and sliced
1 liqueur glass brandy

1 Toss veal in flour and Bisto mixture. Heat butter and oil in pan. Add onion and garlic. Fry until pale gold. Move to edges of pan.
2 Add meat to pan. Fry fairly briskly until well-browned all over.
3 Add tomato purée, wine, tomatoes, salt and bouquet garni. Bring to boil, stirring. Lower heat. Cover.
4 Simmer gently for 1¼ hours when veal should be just tender. Add mushrooms. Continue to cook a further ¼ hour.
5 Heat brandy to lukewarm. Flame with a lit match. Pour into veal mixture. Stir round to mix.

Serve straight away with freshly cooked polenta (below) and spinach.

Polenta (serves 6)
1¼pt (¾ litre) boiling water
2 level tsp salt
7oz (200g) corn meal (polenta)
1oz (25g) butter, plus a little extra
grated Parmesan cheese

1 Pour water and salt into pan. Add corn meal. Cook, stirring, until mixture bubbles and thickens.
2 Add 1oz (25g) of the butter and continue to cook for ¼ hour, stirring frequently to prevent sticking over base of pan.
3 Transfer to a dish and sprinkle with Parmesan cheese. Top with extra flakes of butter and serve piping hot with the veal.

Variations: For important occasions when you want more sophisticated versions of the brandied veal, try the two following recipes.

Brandied Veal with Chestnuts (serves 6)
Follow recipe for brandied veal but instead of mushrooms, add 1 well-drained can (15½oz or 440g) whole chestnuts in water.

Brandied Veal with Artichokes (serves 6)
Follow recipe for brandied veal but instead of mushrooms, add 6 canned artichoke hearts, well drained and halved.

Creamed Veal Veronique (serves 6)

Follow recipe for creamed turkey veronique on page 102 but substitute 2lb (1kg) fillet of veal for the turkey.
In view of the price of veal fillet, regard this as a luxury dish!

Bulgarian Kebap (serves 4 to 6)

A kebap in Bulgaria is a stew, and this one features breast of veal, simmered with a flavoursome assortment of vegetables.

4 tbsp salad oil
8oz (225g) onions, very thinly sliced
3 medium green peppers, de-seeded and cut into strips
3lb (1½kg) boned breast of veal, cut into 1 inch (2½cm) cubes
3 heaped tsp Bisto
1 rounded tsp marjoram
¼pt (150ml) water
1 level tsp salt
1lb (500g) skinned tomatoes, chopped

1 Heat oil in heavy-based pan. Add onions. Fry covered for about ¼ hour or until pale gold. Add peppers. Fry fairly briskly until they turn a dull green. Remove vegetables from oil temporarily.
2 Add breast of veal to remaining oil in pan. Fry over fairly brisk heat until golden. Replace fried vegetables. Stir in all remaining ingredients.

3 Bring to boil, stirring. Lower heat. Cover. Simmer gently 1½ to 2 hours or until veal is soft. Stir occasionally to prevent sticking.
Serve with thick slices of soft crusted bread and green vegetables.

Classic Wiener Schnitzel (serves 4)

This is a costly dish but ideally suited to very special occasions when only the best will do.

4 veal escalopes (also called fillet), each about 3oz (75g)
3 level tbsp flour mixed with1 rounded tsp Onion Bisto
1 × Grades 1 or 2 (large) egg
1 tsp water
about 10 rounded tbsp *lightly* toasted breadcrumbs
corn oil for frying

Garnish
lemon wedges
parsley
capers

1 Ask your butcher to beat each piece of veal until paper-thin. Wash and dry. Snip all the way round the edge of each escalope to prevent it from curling as it cooks.
2 Coat each escalope in flour mixed with Bisto. Dip in egg well beaten with water, then toss in crumbs, making sure there are no thin patches.
3 Leave to stand for ¼ hour to give coating a chance to set, then lift up each escalope and shake off surplus crumbs.
4 Heat oil till hot in large pan. Add escalopes, one or two at a time, so that they are able to float about in the oil. Fry about 8 to 10 minutes.
5 Lift out of pan and drain on crumpled paper towels. Transfer to 1 large or 4 individual warm dinner plates. Garnish each with lemon, parsley and 2 or 3 capers.
Serve Austrian-style with potato salad. Otherwise accompany with fried potatoes and either green vegetables or salad.

Wiener Schnitzel Holstein
Make exactly as classic Wiener Schnitzel but instead of lemon, parsley and caper garnish, top each schnitzel with a freshly fried egg.

Veal Marengo (serves 4 to 6)
Follow recipe for chicken marengo on page 94, but instead of chicken use 2lb (1kg) diced-up pie veal.

Osso Buco (serves 4)

A fragrant and colourful stew from Italy made from cut-up shin of veal. Because veal in general, and this cut in particular, is not readily available, I would suggest you give your butcher advance warning.

4lb (2kg) shin of veal, cut into 3 inch (7½cm) lengths
  (*do not* remove bone)
2 level tbsp flour mixed with 4 rounded tsp Bisto
4 tbsp salad oil
6oz (175g) onion, grated
4oz (125g) carrot, very thinly sliced
2 large celery stalks, thinly sliced
1 can (about 16oz or 450g) tomatoes
2 rounded tbsp tomato purée
½pt (275ml) dry white wine
4 tbsp water
2 large garlic cloves, crushed
salt and pepper to taste

Egg-and-crumbed pork escalope

1 Wash and dry veal, then coat pieces in mixture of flour and Bisto.
2 Heat oil in large pan. Add veal, a few pieces at a time. Fry until well-sealed and brown. Remove to plate temporarily.
3 Add onion, carrot and celery to remaining oil in pan. Fry slowly until light gold.
4 Mix in tomatoes, tomato purée, wine, water and garlic. Bring to boil, stirring. Replace veal. Season to taste. Cover. Simmer 1½ to 2 hours or until meat is tender.
  Serve with rice.

Veal Chops Pizzaiola (serves 4)

Make exactly as steak pizzaiola (page 29), using veal chops instead of steak. Grill or fry the chops, making sure they are well cooked through.

5 Poultry and Game

Poultry is extremely versatile and can be roasted, grilled, fried casseroled and stewed. Prices compare favourably with those of other meats, and poultry has a regular place in most households' buying. The mini-turkey has joined the traditional birds available, and with a drawn weight of as little as 5lb (2½kg), this is an excellent purchase all the year round.

Choosing Poultry

When buying frozen poultry, check that the wrappings are unbroken, and the skin a good colour.

Chicken

A fresh chicken should have an unbroken, straight, pliable breastbone and a plump breast. The flesh should be creamy-white and have no discolouration. Allow about 8oz (225g) raw chicken on the bone per portion.

Turkey

A fresh turkey should have a bright comb, white flesh, smooth legs, a pliable breastbone and no blood discolouration on the neck. Allow approximately 12oz (350g) raw turkey (including bone) per portion. Hen birds are a better buy as they have a higher proportion of flesh to bone.

Duck and duckling

A fresh duck or duckling should have a good creamy colour, and smooth legs with soft webbing which can be easily torn. A 3lb to 4lb (1½ to 2kg) duck (drawn weight) will serve 4 to 5 helpings. A duckling will serve 2.

Storing Poultry

Freshly drawn poultry should be loosely wrapped in greaseproof paper, placed on a plate to catch any drips and kept in the refrigerator, where it may be left for up to 2 days. Frozen poultry should be completely thawed out before cooking. Chicken, goose and duck will take about 24 hours to thaw out in a refrigerator and a large turkey can take up to 3 days. As a guide, allow about 5 hours to each pound (500g) of meat.

The Different Birds

Chicken

Poussins are 4 to 8 week old chickens. Serve one per person. Fresh poussins are available from March to July. They can be roasted or grilled.

Spring chickens are 2 to 4 months old and usually weigh about 2 to 2½lb(1 to 1¼kg), drawn weight. They can be roasted, grilled, fried or baked. Roasters are 6 to 12 months old and weigh about 4 to 6lb (2 to 3kg), drawn. They can be roasted, grilled, baked or fried.

Boiling fowl are 12 months old and over, and of about 4 to 6lb (2 to 3kg) drawn weight. They can be steam-boiled or pot-roasted.

Capons are young cockerels which have been specially reared to produce a higher proportion of flesh to bone. They usually weigh about 5 to 10lb (2½ to 5kg), drawn.

Chicken is also sold as halves, quarters, breasts, drumsticks or wings. It is more economical to buy a whole chicken and cut it into joints than to buy separate joints.

Turkey

A turkey can weigh from about 5lb to 25lb (2½ to 11kg), drawn weight. It is also available as fillets, drumsticks, or boned and rolled joints ready for cooking.

Goose

Goose can ring the change for you at Christmas time—it was, after all, the traditional Christmas dinner in years gone by. Fresh goose is often difficult to get these days, but is 'in season' from October to March, and frozen goose can often be obtained from large or specialised shops throughout the year. Geese are rather fatty and must be cooked at a high temperature to remove excess fat. The meat is dark and rich compared with duck. It is particularly good served stuffed, with apple or cranberry sauce.

Duck

Ducklings are 6 weeks to 3 months old and are available fresh from March to July. Ducks are available all the year round, but are at their best from July to February. Duckling joints or half-ducks can also be bought, and are available frozen through the year.

Trussing with a skewer

It is necessary to truss a bird to keep it in shape when it has been stuffed, or it will lose its form during cooking and will not look so good when you serve it. Turn the bird breast down, and close the neck opening by folding the loose neck skin over the hole, and folding the wings over this skin to hold it in

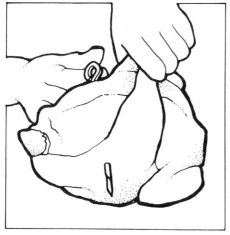

Trussing poultry: push through skewer

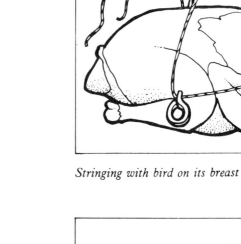

Stringing with bird on its breast

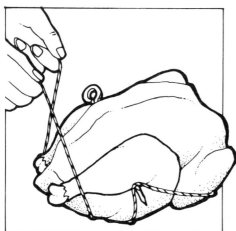

Finish trussing like this

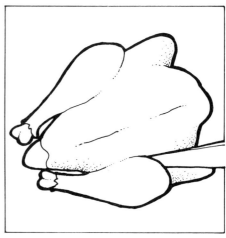

Carving poultry: remove wing and leg

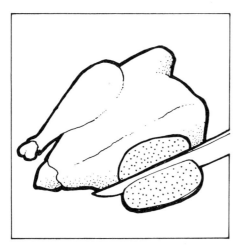

Carve breast both sides

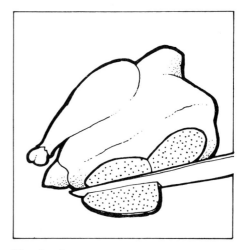

Use slanting cuts

Jointing poultry: pull leg away

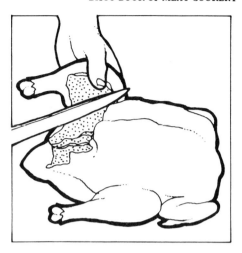

Detach leg from carcase

position. Now slit the skin above the rear end of the bird and push the parson's nose through it.

Then turn the bird on its back, push the legs upwards towards the neck and skewer the bird from side to side, so that the skewer comes out below the thigh bone. Now turn the bird on to its breast; run a piece of string over the wing tips and over the skewer ends. Turn the bird over again on to its back, loop the string round, run it round the drumsticks and parson's nose, and tie it securely.

Jointing

Chicken and duck can be halved or jointed. Place small birds on their backs and halve them by cutting straight down through the breastbone and then through the backbone.

Larger birds can be further divided into joints. To joint a leg, push the knife blade underneath the joint and slice it away from the wing, drawing the leg away from the bird as you slice. If you want to joint a chicken completely, pull the leg away from the body and detach it where the thigh joins the carcase. Next cut the wing joint by cutting down from the breast towards the wing: fold the breast meat over the wing. Separate the top of the breast from the rest of the bird by cutting along the break in the rib cage. Then divide the top portion. Divide the breast portion into two pieces. Use the carcase for making stock.

Carving Poultry

First cut through the skin of wing and leg, and remove them from the carcase. Then start carving at the breast. Carve both sides until you are down to the breastbone, making your slices in slanting cuts to get them longer. The legs can be carved along the length of the leg bone, or, if it is a small bird, be served as individual portions.

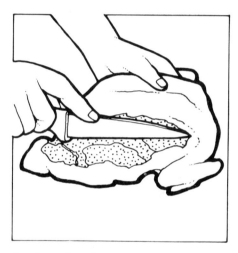

Cut down from breast to cut wing joint

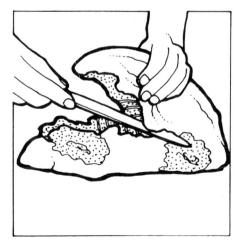

Separate top of breast by cutting along break in ribcage

Roast Chicken

Allow 20 minutes per pound (500g) at 400°F (200°C), Gas 6. Serve with the same accompaniments as roast turkey: bread sauce, bacon rolls, chipolata sausages, gravy and, if liked, parsley and thyme stuffing.

Allow about 10 to 12oz (275 to 350g) raw weight per person.

Freezing

Cooked chicken, or made-up chicken dishes, can be frozen for up to six months.

Note

If the chicken is frozen, it must be thoroughly thawed before cooking.

Chicken Hawaii (serves 8)

1 × 4lb (2kg) chicken, freshly roasted
2oz (50g) butter or margarine
4oz (125g) onion, chopped
1 garlic clove, crushed
2oz (50g) flour
3 heaped tsp Bisto
1 to 2 level tbsp mild curry powder
1pt (575ml) chicken stock, made from giblets and
  chicken cube
1 fresh pineapple (2lb or 1kg)
1 carton (5oz or 142ml) natural yogurt
¼pt (150ml) single cream
salt and pepper to taste

1 Cut chicken into bite-size pieces, discarding skin and bones. Leave on one side temporarily.
2 Heat butter or margarine in large pan. Add onion and garlic. Cover. Fry gently for 10 minutes.
3 Stir in flour, Bisto and curry powder. Gradually blend in stock. Cook, stirring, until sauce comes to boil and thickens.
4 Add chicken. Leave to simmer over low heat for 10 minutes.
5 Meanwhile peel pineapple and cut flesh into small cubes. Add to pan of chicken.

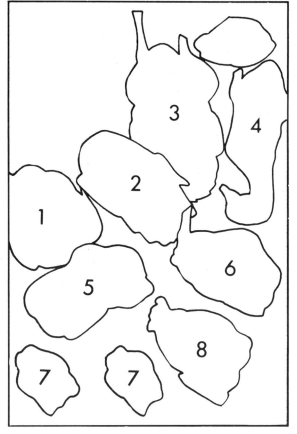

Poultry, ready trussed:
1 *turkey* **2** *goose* **3** *turkey* **4, 5** *duck* **6** *capon* **7** *poussin* **8** *chicken—a roaster*

6 Stir in yogurt and cream. Heat till very hot. Adjust seasoning to taste.

Serve with rice and a side-dish of desiccated coconut for sprinkling over the top.

Chicken Hawaii

Croatian cream chicken with rum

Grilled Chicken Espagnole (serves 4)

½pt (250ml) gravy made with Bisto Rich Gravy
  Granules and water as directed
2oz (50g) trimmed mushrooms, sliced with stalks
1 level tbsp very finely chopped parsley
2oz (50g) onion, grated
2 medium skinned tomatoes, chopped
2 heaped tsp tomato purée
1 small garlic clove, crushed (optional)
4 medium chicken joints (thawed if frozen)
2oz (50g) butter or margarine, melted
salt and pepper to taste

1 Pour gravy into pan. Add the mushrooms, parsley, grated onion, tomatoes, tomato purée and garlic, slowly bringing to boil. Cover. Lower heat. Simmer about 30 minutes while chicken is grilling.
2 Stand chicken in grill pan, skin side uppermost. Brush with butter or margarine. Sprinkle with salt and pepper to taste. Grill about 30 to 40 minutes.
3 Turn often and brush with butter or margarine every time. Also remember to sprinkle with salt and pepper.
4 Blend sauce till smooth in blender goblet. Reheat until bubbling. Adjust seasoning.
5 Spoon over chicken.
  Serve with fried potatoes and a green salad.

Croatian Cream Chicken with Rum (serves 6)

A novelty chicken dish from Yugoslavia.

1 × 4lb (2kg) oven-ready chicken, freshly roasted
¾pt (425ml) chicken stock (either made from giblets
  or a cube and water)
4 egg yolks

5 tbsp mild malt vinegar
3 level tsp Onion Bisto
1½ level tbsp Dijon mustard
1 level tsp soft brown sugar
1 tbsp dark rum
2 cartons (*each* 5oz or 142ml) soured cream
salt and pepper to taste

1 Cut chicken into serving-size pieces. Transfer to a large serving dish and keep hot.
2 Place the stock, egg yolks, vinegar and Bisto in a double pan, or a basin standing over a pan of gently simmering water.
3 Cook, whisking continuously, until sauce just comes up to the boil and thickens sufficiently to cling to the whisk.
4 Beat in rest of ingredients. Whisk again until very hot. Season to taste. Spoon half the sauce over the chicken; pour the other half into a sauce boat and pass separately.
  Accompany with pasta and courgettes or beans.

Israeli Orange Chicken (serves 4)

1 × 3lb (1½kg) oven-ready chicken, thawed if frozen,
  and jointed
1 level tsp salt
1 large garlic clove, crushed
2 level tsp paprika
½ level tsp mixed herbs
½ level tsp *each* finely grated lemon and orange peels
strained juice of a small lemon
unstrained juice of 2 medium oranges
4 tbsp water
2 heaped tsp Onion Bisto
1 extra tbsp cold water
salt and pepper to taste

Pacific island chicken

1 Place chicken into saucepan. Mix salt with garlic, paprika, herbs, grated peels and fruit juices.
2 Pour over chicken with water. Bring slowly to boil. Lower heat. Cover. Bubble gently for ¾ hour.
3 Mix Onion Bisto smoothly with water. Pour over chicken. Boil slowly till thickened. Adjust seasoning.
   Serve with boiled potatoes and salad.

Chicken Teriyaki-style (serves 4 to 6)

1 × 3lb (1½kg) oven-ready chicken, thawed if frozen, and jointed
3 tbsp soy sauce
2 level tbsp caster sugar
4 tbsp dry sherry
1 piece of preserved ginger, thinly sliced
1 tbsp ginger syrup
2 large garlic cloves, crushed
1 heaped tsp Onion Bisto
2 tbsp cold water
1 small can (about 8oz or 225g) bamboo shoots, drained
1 small can (about 8oz or 225g) water chestnuts, drained and sliced
salt and white pepper to taste

1 Place chicken into fairly large pan which is shallow rather than deep.
2 Combine soy sauce with the sugar, sherry, ginger syrup and garlic. Pour over chicken. Bring to boil very gently. Lower heat. Cover.
3 Simmer about ¾ hour or till chicken is tender. To thicken slightly, mix Bisto with cold water. Stir into chicken.
4 Add bamboo shoots and water chestnuts. Season to taste. Bubble gently 2 to 3 minutes.
   Serve with rice.

Pacific Island Chicken (serves 6)

1 × 3lb (1½kg) oven-ready chicken, thawed if frozen, and jointed
2 level tsp cornflour mixed with 2 rounded tsp Onion Bisto
1oz (25g) butter
2 tsp salad oil
1 can (6¼ fluid oz or 178ml) frozen concentrated orange juice, thawed but left undiluted
1 tbsp fresh lime or lemon juice
½ level tsp salt
½ level tsp cinnamon
2 large bananas, sliced
2oz (50g) brazil nuts, thinly sliced
3 heaped tbsp desiccated coconut, lightly toasted under grill

1 Coat chicken joints with cornflour and Bisto mixture. Heat butter and oil in large frying pan till sizzling.
2 Add chicken joints. Fry briskly until brown all over, turning twice.
3 Stir in next 4 ingredients. Cover pan. Bubble gently for about ¾ hour or until chicken is tender. Stir in bananas and nuts. Heat through 3 minutes.
4 Turn into a serving dish and sprinkle with toasted coconut.
   Accompany with rice.

Mallorcan Red-Pepper Chicken (serves 6)

1 × 4lb (2kg) oven-ready chicken, thawed if frozen, and jointed
6oz (175g) onions, chopped
1 large garlic clove, crushed
5 tbsp salad oil
6 medium-sized red peppers, de-seeded and cut into thin strips
12oz (350g) mild ham, cut into very small dice
4 rounded tsp Bisto
1½lb (750g) skinned tomatoes, de-seeded and chopped
salt and pepper to taste

1 Wash and dry chicken. Leave on one side temporarily. Meanwhile fry onions and garlic gently in the oil until soft and pale gold.
2 Add chicken joints. Fry a little more briskly until golden-brown all over. Take out and leave on a plate.
3 Add peppers and ham to onions and garlic in pan. Cover. Fry slowly ¼ hour. Stir in Bisto and tomatoes. Season to taste.
4 Replace chicken. Bring slowly to boil. Lower heat. Cover. Simmer ¾ hour when chicken should be tender. Stir occasionally.
  Serve hot with rice and salad.

Chicken Cacciatora (serves 4 to 6)

1 × 4lb (2kg) oven-ready chicken, thawed if frozen, and jointed
1oz (25g) flour mixed with 3 rounded tsp Bisto
1oz (25g) butter
2 tbsp salad oil
2 medium onions, chopped
2 large garlic cloves, crushed
1lb (500g) skinned tomatoes, chopped
3 rounded tbsp tomato purée
1 level tsp caster sugar
¼pt (150ml) water
salt and pepper to taste
8oz (225g) trimmed mushrooms, sliced
4 tbsp medium sherry

1 Coat chicken pieces thoroughly with flour and Bisto mixture.
2 Heat butter and oil in large pan. Add chicken. Fry until joints are brown all over. Remove to plate temporarily.
3 Add onions and garlic to remaining butter and oil in pan. Fry over medium heat until pale gold. Stir in tomatoes, purée, sugar, water and salt and pepper to taste.
4 Replace chicken. Cover. Simmer about ¾ hour or until chicken is just tender, stirring occasionally.
5 Add mushrooms and sherry, mix in well and cook a further ¼ hour.
  Serve with pasta or rice and a green salad.

Chicken Marengo (serves 4 to 6)

This is another Italian speciality which is similar to the cacciatora. To make, follow recipe for chicken cacciatora but add 2 level tbsp tomato purée, 3 heaped tbsp chopped parsley and 2oz (50g) black olives with the salt and pepper. Add 3 to 4oz (75 to 100g) mushrooms and 5 tbsp dry white wine instead of the sherry.

Chinese Chicken Stew (serves 4)

1 small chicken, thawed if frozen, divided into 4 joints
1 level tbsp flour
4 rounded tsp Onion Bisto
3 tbsp salad oil
1pt (575ml) water
3 pieces stem ginger (in syrup), drained and chopped
4oz (125g) button mushrooms, trimmed
1 can (11oz or 300g) Chinese-style vegetables (or 1 small can *each* bean sprouts and bamboo shoots)
salt and pepper to taste

1 Wash chicken and wipe dry with paper towels. Coat all over with flour and Onion Bisto, well mixed together.
2 Heat oil in large and heavy-based pan. Add chicken. Fry until crisp-looking and golden.
3 Add all remaining ingredients, including any left-over flour and Onion Bisto mixture.
4 Bring to boil, stirring. Lower heat. Cover. Simmer ¾ hour to 1 hour when chicken should be tender.
  Serve with Chinese-style noodles.

Coq au Vin (serves 4)

1 × 3lb (1½kg) oven-ready chicken, thawed if frozen, and jointed
1 level tbsp flour mixed with 3 rounded tsp Bisto
1oz (25g) butter
2 tbsp salad oil
4oz (100 to 125g) unsmoked lean bacon, coarsely chopped
8oz (225g) onions, chopped
2oz (50g) carrots, thinly sliced
1 large garlic clove, crushed
12 shallots, peeled and left whole
1 bouquet garni
3 rounded tbsp chopped parsley
1 to 2 level tsp salt
½pt (275ml) dry red wine
8oz (225g) trimmed mushrooms, sliced
pepper to taste

1 Coat chicken with flour and Bisto mixture. Heat butter and oil in large and heavy-based pan. Add chicken. Fry until well-browned all over. Remove to a plate.

Sweet-and-sour pork

2 Add bacon, onions, carrots and garlic to remaining butter and oil in pan. Fry about 10 minutes or until lightly browned. Add all remaining ingredients except mushrooms and pepper.

3 Bring to boil, stirring. Replace chicken, making sure it is well-basted with pan juices. Lower heat. Cover. Simmer gently for 1 hour.

4 Add mushrooms. Season to taste with pepper. Cook further ¼ hour.

Serve hot with boiled potatoes and green vegetables to taste.

Chicken Paprika (serves 6)
Follow recipe for creamy paprika veal on page 84 but use 6 chicken joints instead of the veal. Omit bacon and substitute an equal quantity of button mushrooms. Use 1 green pepper instead of 2.

Chicken Curry (serves 4)

2oz (50g) butter
2 tsp salad oil
1 × 3lb (1½kg) oven-ready chicken, thawed if frozen, and jointed
8oz (225g) onions, chopped
1 large garlic clove, crushed
3 level tbsp Madras curry powder (mild, medium or hot, depending on taste)
3 heaped tsp Bisto
3 level tbsp tomato purée
1 tbsp lemon juice
1 large bay leaf
1 bouquet garni
3 level tbsp peach chutney
½ level tsp *each* ground cinnamon, ginger and grated nutmeg
½pt (275ml) water
1oz (25g) creamed coconut, cut from block
salt and pepper to taste

Accompaniments or sambals
Side dishes of:

mango chutney
sliced onions topped with sliced tomatoes
coarsely chopped peanuts
natural yogurt
diced cucumber

1 Heat butter and oil in heavy-based pan. Add chicken joints and fry until golden all over. Remove to plate.
2 Add onions and garlic to remaining butter and oil in pan. Fry over medium heat till golden.
3 Stir in all remaining ingredients except creamed coconut and seasoning. Bring to boil. Replace chicken. Baste with curry sauce.
4 Lower heat. Cover. Simmer 1 hour when chicken should be tender. Add small pieces of creamed coconut and stir until melted. Adjust seasoning to taste.
   Serve with freshly cooked Basmati rice and accompany with sambals, as suggested above.

Turkey Curry

Follow recipe for chicken curry but substitute 2lb (1kg) boned and diced turkey for the chicken. If the bird is very tender, ¾ hour cooking time may be adequate.

Austrian Fried Chicken (Backhendl) (serves 4)

Follow recipe for Chicken Maryland but fry 4 chicken joints (in deep pan) in plenty of salad oil or lard until crisp and golden. Drain on paper towels and serve hot with boiled potatoes tossed round and round in butter and chopped parsley.
   Lemon wedges and watercress are the customary garnishes for the chicken.

Chicken Maryland (serves 4)

An American speciality, traditionally served with corn fritters and butter-fried bananas.

4 joints roasting chicken (1½lb or 750g), thawed if frozen
3 level tbsp flour mixed with 3 level tsp Bisto
2 × Grade 3 (standard) eggs
2 tbsp milk
4 heaped tbsp lightly toasted breadcrumbs
salad oil for frying

Garnish
watercress

1 Wash and dry chicken, then coat all over with flour and Bisto mixture.
2 In fairly deep plate, beat eggs and milk well together. Dip in chicken joints, then toss in crumbs. Leave to stand for a minimum of ¼ hour for coating to harden.
3 Heat about 1 inch (2½cm) oil, for ¼ hour, in large and shallow casserole by placing in oven set to 400°F (200°C), Gas 6.
4 Place chicken joints into casserole. Turn over with 2 spoons so that both sides are coated with fat.
5 Return to oven and 'oven-fry' for about 35 to 45 minutes or until chicken is brown and crisp. Do not cover.
6 Before serving, remove from casserole and drain on paper towels.
   Serve hot with the fritters and fried bananas.

Bacon and egg casserole

Corn Fritters
4oz (125g) self-raising flour
½ level tsp powder mustard
¼ level tsp salt
1 × Grade 3 (standard) egg
¼pt (150ml) milk
4 tbsp canned sweet corn, well-drained
a little white cooking fat, melted

1 Sift flour, mustard and salt into bowl. Gradually mix to a batter with unbeaten egg and the milk.
2 Beat vigorously until smooth and creamy. Stir in corn.
3 Brush a heavy-based and smooth-faced pan with melted fat. Heat until very hot. Drop rounds of fritter batter, from a tablespoon, into pan.
4 Fry until golden. Turn over. Fry second side till golden. Pile in a napkin as fritters are cooked, to keep warm and moist.

Fried Bananas
Allow 1 medium banana per person. Peel. Cut in half lengthwise. Fry gently in butter until golden on both sides. Serve hot.

Maryland Casserole (serves 4)

1 medium onion, sliced
6 rashers streaky bacon, chopped
1 tbsp salad oil
8 chicken wings or thighs
1 level tbsp flour, seasoned with salt and pepper
4 rounded tsp Bisto
1pt (575ml) water
¼ level tsp rosemary
1 can (11½oz or about 315g) sweet corn
2 medium bananas

1 Fry onion and bacon in oil for 4 minutes. Drain well and transfer to a casserole.
2 Toss chicken in seasoned flour and fry in same oil to brown evenly. Put into casserole.
3 Mix Bisto smoothly with a little of the cold water. Blend in remaining water and pour over chicken. Add rosemary.
4 Cover and cook in the centre of the oven set to 350°F (180°C), Gas 4, for 1 hour until chicken joints are tender.
5 Remove casserole from oven, stir in drained sweet corn and arrange sliced bananas on top. Cook for a further 15 minutes.

Caribbean Chicken (serves 4)

1 × 3lb (1½kg) oven-ready chicken, thawed if frozen
1oz (25g) flour
3 heaped tsp Bisto
1 level tsp extra hot curry powder
1 level tsp powder mustard
1 level tsp salt
½ level tsp mixed spice
2 tbsp salad oil
1 large onion, chopped
1 large celery stalk, thinly sliced
4oz (125g) mushrooms and stalks, trimmed and sliced
¼pt (150ml) orange juice
¼pt (150ml) water
3 tbsp dark rum
pepper to taste

1 Cut chicken into 8 joints.
2 Mix together flour, Bisto, curry powder, mustard, salt and mixed spice.
3 Coat chicken joints heavily with flour mixture and leave on one side temporarily.
4 Heat oil in pan. Add chicken joints. Fry until golden brown. Remove to plate.
5 Add onion and celery to remaining oil in pan. Fry gently until pale gold. Stir in mushrooms. Fry 5 minutes.
6 Pour in orange juice, water, rum and pepper to taste. Bring to boil, stirring.
7 Replace chicken. Cover. Simmer gently for about ¾ to 1 hour or until chicken is tender.
   Serve with sweet corn and yams (sweet potatoes) when available. As an alternative to yams, try macaroni.

Mexican Chocolate Chicken (serves 6)

Mexico, home of chocolate, uses it to good advantage in this richly brown chicken stew, which is lightly spiced with cinnamon and peppered with cayenne.

4lb (2kg) oven-ready chicken, thawed if frozen, and jointed
1½ level tbsp cornflour mixed with 3 rounded tsp Bisto
2oz (50g) butter or margarine
2 tsp salad oil
6oz (175g) onion, finely chopped or grated
3 level tbsp tomato purée
¾pt (425ml) water
½ level tsp cayenne pepper
1 large de-seeded green pepper, cut into strips
bouquet garni
2oz (50g) plain chocolate, coarsely chopped
1 level tsp cinnamon or 3 inch (7½cm) stick of cinnamon
salt to taste

1 Coat chicken joints with cornflour-and-Bisto mixture.
2 Heat butter or margarine with salad oil in large pan until foamy. Add chicken. Fry until crisp and brown all over. Remove to plate.
3 Add onion to remaining butter and oil in pan. Fry gently until pale gold. Stir in rest of ingredients. Bring slowly to boil, stirring.

4 Replace chicken. Cover. Simmer over low heat ¾ to 1 hour or until tender. Stir occasionally.

Serve with rice or pasta and green vegetables to taste.

Chicken in Devilled Sauce (serves 4)

4 medium chicken joints, thawed if frozen
2 level tbsp flour
3 heaped tsp Onion Bisto
⅛ to ¼ level tsp cayenne pepper (fiery, so be careful)
3 tbsp salad oil
4 level tbsp tomato ketchup
2 level tbsp Demerara sugar
3 tbsp malt vinegar
1 level tsp prepared English mustard
3 tsp Worcestershire sauce
1 tbsp fresh lime juice (or 2 tsp lime cordial)
¼pt (150ml) boiling water
salt and pepper to taste

1 Mix together flour, Onion Bisto and cayenne pepper.
2 Coat chicken joints thickly with the flour mixture. Heat oil in large pan. Add chicken. Fry on both sides till golden and crisp.
3 Add rest of ingredients to pan. Slowly bring to boil, stirring. Lower heat. Cover. Simmer gently ¾ to 1 hour or until chicken is tender.

Serve with freshly cooked brown rice and broccoli tossed in butter and sprinkled with powdered mace.

Chicken and Vegetable Braise (serves 4)

1 × 3lb (1½kg) oven-ready chicken, thawed if frozen
2 level tsp Bisto
cold water
2 tbsp salad oil
8oz (225g) onions, halved
8oz (225g) carrots, cut into 1 inch (2½cm) lengths
1lb (500g) potatoes, cut into even-sized pieces
1 bouquet garni
salt and pepper to taste
1 rounded tbsp flour
1 level tbsp tomato ketchup

1 Remove giblets from chicken. Wash thoroughly. Cook, covered, with enough water to cover for ¾ hour. Strain, reserving stock. Blend Bisto smoothly with 1 or 2 tbsp cold water. Add to stock.
2 Heat salad oil in large pan. Add chicken and brown well all over. Transfer to fairly spacious casserole.
3 Add onions and carrots to remaining oil in pan. Fry about 5 minutes. Add potatoes, bouquet garni, Bisto stock and salt and pepper to taste. Bring slowly to boil.

4 Pour into casserole and cover. Cook 1 to 1½ hours in oven set to 375°F (190°C), Gas 5. Transfer chicken carefully to a warm serving dish and surround with vegetables. Keep hot.
5 Mix flour smoothly with 1 tbsp cold water. Stir in tomato ketchup and Bisto juices from casserole. Bring to boil in saucepan, stirring. Adjust seasoning to taste.
6 Pour some sauce over the chicken. Pass remainder in gravy boat.

Accompany with boiled potatoes.

Madeira Chicken (serves 4 to 6)

1oz (25g) butter
2 tsp salad oil
1 × 4lb (2kg) oven-ready chicken, thawed if frozen, and jointed
1 small turnip, diced
1 small parsnip, diced
2 medium carrots, sliced
1 medium garlic clove, chopped
4oz (100 to 125g) button mushrooms, trimmed but left whole
1 tbsp finely chopped parsley
¼ level tsp tarragon
1 level tsp salt
¼pt (125ml) Madeira
¼pt (125ml) water
1 level tsp cornflour
3 heaped tsp Onion Bisto
3 tbsp cold water

1 Heat butter and oil in heavy-based pan. Add chicken. Fry until golden-brown all over. Remove to plate. Leave on one side temporarily.
2 Add next 10 ingredients to pan. Bring slowly to boil. Replace chicken. Lower heat. Cover. Simmer very gently for 1 to 1½ hours or until chicken is tender.
3 To thicken, mix cornflour and Bisto smoothly with water. Pour into pan. Cook, stirring gently, until bubbly. Simmer 1 minute.

Serve with freshly cooked rice forked with butter, and green vegetables to taste.

Chicken and Mushroom Casserole (serves 4 to 6)

2oz (50g) butter or margarine
2 large onions, sliced
6 large chicken drumsticks, thawed if frozen
1 rounded tsp Bisto mixed with 1 rounded tbsp flour
8oz (225g) potatoes, peeled and grated
¾pt (425ml) water
1 bouquet garni
salt and pepper to taste
2oz (50g) mushrooms, sliced

1 Melt butter or margarine in pan, add onions and fry for 3 minutes.
2 Toss drumsticks in Bisto-and-flour mixture. Add to onions in pan and brown evenly.
3 Put onions and drumsticks into a casserole with the potatoes.
4 Pour in the water. Add bouquet garni with salt and pepper. Cover.
5 Cook for 1 hour at 350°F (180°C), Gas 4.
6 Add mushrooms and return to oven for a further 15 minutes.

Hunter's Chicken Casserole (serves 4)

1 large onion, coarsely chopped
4oz (100 to 125g) lean bacon, cubed
2 tbsp salad oil
4 medium-sized chicken joints, thawed if frozen
4 level tsp Bisto
¼pt (150ml) water
½pt (250ml) dry red wine
salt and pepper to taste
3 medium carrots, thickly sliced
4oz (100 to 125g) button mushrooms, trimmed

1 Fry onion and bacon cubes in the oil until pale gold. Keep pan covered, heat low and allow about 15 to 20 minutes.
2 Add chicken joints. Increase heat and fry a little more briskly until well-browned on all sides.
3 Mix Bisto smoothly with a few tbsp of water. Blend in rest of water and wine. Season.
4 Transfer onion, bacon and chicken joints to ovenproof casserole. Add carrots.
5 Pour Bisto liquid into casserole. Cover with lid. Cook 1½ hours in oven at 350°F (180°C), Gas 4. Uncover. Add mushrooms.
6 Cover again and return casserole to oven for a further 20 minutes.
   Serve with whole boiled potatoes and green vegetables to taste.

Tip
Halved wood-pigeons may be used instead of chicken.

Farmhouse Chicken Stew (serves 6)

1 boiling fowl (about 3lb or 1½kg), thawed if frozen
12oz (350g) small whole carrots
12oz (350g) small whole potatoes
3 medium celery stalks, chopped
8oz (225g) button onions or shallots
2 split and well-washed medium leeks, cut into 2 inch (5cm) lengths
6 large parsley sprigs
1 medium bay leaf
1 level tsp coarsely ground white or black pepper
4 rounded tsp Bisto
2pt (1¼ litres) water

1 Put the chicken into a large pan with the carrots, potatoes, celery, onions or shallots, leeks, parsley sprigs, bay leaf and pepper.
2 Mix the Bisto to a smooth paste with a little of the water. Blend in remaining water.
3 Pour the Bisto liquid over the chicken and vegetables.
4 Cover the pan and simmer gently for 1¾ hours.

Tip
If you prefer vegetables that are less well cooked, add them halfway through the cooking time.

Roast Turkey

Allow 15 minutes per pound (500g) for birds up to 14lb (6¼kg) drawn weight, 10 minutes per pound (500g) for birds over 14lb (7kg). Accompany with bread sauce, bacon rolls, chipolata sausages, assorted vegetables to taste, roast and/or boiled potatoes and Bisto gravy. Choose any stuffing to taste (packet stuffing-mix or homemade) or try chestnut stuffing (recipe below).

   The amounts to allow per person are:

12oz (350g) raw weight for small and medium-sized turkeys
8oz (225g) raw weight for large turkeys of about 16lb (8kg) or over

Freezing

Made-up dishes or pieces of cooked turkey can be frozen for up to 6 months.

Note
If the turkey is frozen it must be well thawed before cooking—allow about 5 hours thawing time per pound (500g).

Hunter's chicken casserole

Chestnut stuffing(sufficient for an 8lb (3¾kg) turkey)
4 rashers streaky bacon, de-rinded and chopped
1 small onion, grated
1 can (about 1lb or 450g size) canned chestnut purée
  (unsweetened)
salt and pepper to taste

1 Fry bacon very gently in a saucepan till the fat runs. Add onion. Fry a further 5 minutes.
2 Stir chestnut purée into bacon and onion pan, mixing thoroughly. Season to taste then leave until cold before using.

Bread sauce (serves 8 to 10)
1 small onion, coarsely chopped
3 cloves
1 small bay leaf
½pt (275ml) milk
¼ level tsp salt
shake or two of white pepper
2oz (50g) fresh white breadcrumbs
knob of butter

1 Put onion, cloves, bay leaf, milk and salt and pepper into pan. Bring just up to boil. Lower heat. Simmer gently for 10 minutes.
2 Strain. Return to pan. Stir in crumbs and butter. Stir over low heat till thickened but still creamy.
3 Spoon into a gravy boat or small dish and sprinkle top lightly with grated nutmeg.

Creamed Turkey Veronique (serves 6)

2lb (1kg) turkey breast fillets
2 level tbsp flour
4 heaped tsp Bisto
1 rounded tsp paprika
½ level tsp powder mustard
2oz (50g) butter
2 tbsp salad oil
1 medium onion, finely chopped
½pt (275ml) water
¼pt (150ml) dry sherry
¼ level tsp tarragon
3 rounded tbsp thick mayonnaise
1 carton (5oz or 142ml) soured cream
1 heaped tbsp finely chopped parsley
4oz (100 to 125g) skinned green grapes, halved and
  with pips removed

1 Mix together flour, Bisto, paprika and mustard powder.
2 Coat turkey fillets all over with flour mixture.
3 Heat butter and oil until sizzling. Add turkey and fry briskly on all sides until golden-brown. Remove to plate.
4 Add onion to remaining fat in pan, together with any leftover flour mixture. Fry, with lid on pan, about 10 minutes or until soft but still pale in colour.

5 Stir in water, sherry and tarragon. Replace turkey. Simmer about ½ hour or until turkey is tender.
6 Beat together mayonnaise, soured cream and parsley. Add to turkey. Bring just up to boil, stirring.
7 Remove from heat, add grapes and mix in well.
   Serve hot with freshly boiled rice forked with butter and some finely chopped toasted almonds. Accompany with a delicate salad made from lettuce hearts tossed in a mild French dressing.

Turkey Rissoles (serves 4)

An excellent way of using up leftover turkey, especially at Christmas time or Easter.

12oz (350g) cold cooked turkey
3 heaped tsp Onion Bisto
2 × Grade 3 (standard) eggs, lightly beaten
pepper to taste
flour
about 1oz (25g) butter or margarine for frying

1 Finely mince turkey. Put into bowl. Add Bisto, beaten eggs and pepper.
2 Knead with finger tips to form a paste. Divide into 8 pieces. Shape into flat rounds.
3 Coat lightly with flour. Fry in hot butter or margarine for about 8 minutes, turning once.
   Serve hot with chips, vegetables and Bisto gravy, or cold with salad.

Grilled Turkey Rissoles (serves 4)
Grill rissoles in lightly greased grill pan, allowing about 6 minutes and turning twice.

Curried Turkey Rissoles (serves 4)
Add 1 heaped tsp curry paste to the turkey with the other ingredients.

Roast Duck
Allow 15 minutes per pound (500g) plus 15 minutes extra, at 400°F (200°C), Gas 6. Use sage-and-onion stuffing, if liked. Accompany with apple sauce, roast and/or boiled potatoes, green peas and Bisto gravy flavoured with a dash of sherry.
   Allow 1lb (500g) raw weight per person.

Freezing
Made-up dishes or pieces of roast duck can be frozen for up to 6 months.

Roast Duck with Orange Sauce (serves 4)

Follow instructions for roasting a duck. When cooked, place on warm serving dish and keep hot.

Orange Sauce To make this sauce, pour off all but 1 tbsp of fat from roasting tin. Stand tin over medium heat. Stir in 1 level tbsp flour, 3 level tsp Bisto, 1 level tsp sugar, ½pt (275ml) stock made from giblets, the finely grated peel and juice of 1 medium orange, and 1 level tsp finely grated lemon peel. Bring to boil, stirring continuously. Simmer 2 minutes. Stir in 2 tbsp Cointreau or Grand Marnier. Pour into a gravy boat.

Serve with the duck, which should be attractively garnished with fresh orange slices and sprigs of watercress.

Duck Granada (serves 4)

1 × 4lb (2kg) duck, cut into 4 joints
1 level tbsp flour mixed with 3 rounded tsp Onion Bisto
½oz (25g) butter
2 tsp salad oil
4oz (100 to 125g) unsmoked gammon
4oz (100 to 125g) trimmed button mushrooms, left whole with stalks
2 large garlic cloves, chopped
½pt (275ml) rosé wine
¼pt (150ml) fresh orange juice
4oz (100 to125g) stuffed olives, sliced
bouquet garni
1 can (about 1lb or 500g size) peeled tomatoes
salt and pepper to taste

1 Coat duck joints all over with flour and Bisto mixture.
2 Heat butter and oil in strong-based saucepan. Add duck. Fry fairly briskly until golden and crisp. Remove to plate.
3 Add gammon, mushrooms with stalks and garlic cloves to remaining butter and oil in pan. Fry gently until soft, about ¼ hour.
4 Add wine, orange juice, bouquet garni and tomatoes with juice from can. Bring to boil, stirring. Season.
5 Replace duck, turning it round in the sauce. Cover. Simmer gently about 1 hour or until duckling is tender.
6 Leave overnight. Next day, remove fat then reheat by boiling gently ¼ hour.

Serve with boiled rice and green vegetables to taste.

Duck Granada

Creamy French-style rabbit

Red Cherry Duckling (serves 4)

1 × 4lb (2kg) oven-ready duckling, thawed if frozen
salt
3oz (75g) onion, very finely chopped
3 rounded tsp Bisto
1 rounded tsp cornflour
½pt (275ml) medium sherry
2 level tbsp finely chopped parsley
1 level tbsp chopped fresh basil or 1 level tsp dried
2 level tsp tomato purée
4oz (125g) fresh red cherries, halved and sliced

1 Place duckling on roasting rack, skin all over with a fork and sprinkle heavily with salt. Roast 2 hours in oven set to 375°F (190°C), Gas 5. Remove to plate. Keep hot.
2 Pour away all but 2 tbsp duckling fat from roasting tin. Transfer to saucepan. Stand over low heat. Stir in onion, Bisto and cornflour.
3 Gradually blend in sherry. Cook, stirring, till sauce comes to boil and thickens. Add all remaining ingredients. Heat through 5 minutes, stirring continuously.
4 Carve duck into 4 portions. Coat with sauce.
    Serve with freshly creamed potatoes and green vegetables.

Roast Goose

Allow 20 minutes per pound (500g) at 375°F (190°C), Gas 5. If liked, use sage-and-onion stuffing. Serve with exactly the same accompaniments as roast duck but include also redcurrant jelly. For a more flavourful gravy, use Onion Bisto instead of plain.

Freezing

Made-up dishes or portions of cooked goose may be frozen for up to 6 months.

Creamy French-style Rabbit in Mustard Sauce (serves 4)

4 medium joints of *young* rabbit
cold water
lemon juice
1 tbsp salad oil
2oz (50g) onions, finely chopped
1oz (25g) flour
3 heaped tsp Bisto
1 large garlic clove, crushed
½pt (275ml) Anjou rosé wine
1 level tbsp Meaux mustard
2 level tsp tomato purée
1 carton (5oz or 141ml) soured cream
salt and pepper to taste

1 To reduce strong flavour, soak rabbit for 1 hour in cold water to cover. Add a dash of lemon juice. Remove from water. Rinse and dry. Heat oil in pan. Add rabbit. Fry till well browned. Remove to plate.
2 Add onions to rest of oil in pan. Fry very gently, with lid on pan, until the palest gold. Stir in flour, Bisto and garlic.
3 Gradually blend in wine. Cook, stirring, until mixture comes to the boil and thickens. Add mustard and tomato purée.
4 Replace rabbit. Stir well. Cover. Simmer gently about ¾ hour or until tender, stirring occasionally.
5 Add cream, a little at a time, then heat until mixture just begins to bubble. Adjust seasoning to taste.
    Serve with boiled potatoes and a green salad tossed with French dressing.

Jugged rabbit

French-style Chicken in Mustard Sauce (serves 4)

Make exactly as the French-style rabbit above, but substitute 4 medium portions of chicken for the rabbit. Do not soak in water and lemon juice.

Rich Rabbit Stew (serves 4)

1 large onion, sliced
1oz (25g) butter or margarine
2 tbsp salad oil
4 large rabbit joints
1oz (25g) flour
1 tbsp tomato purée
4 heaped tsp Bisto
1pt (575ml) water
2 heaped tbsp chopped parsley
salt and pepper to taste
8oz (225g) cocktail-sized frankfurters

1 Fry onion in butter or margarine and oil for 4 minutes.
2 Dust rabbit joints in flour.
3 Add to onion and fry until lightly browned on all sides. Stir in tomato purée.
4 Blend Bisto to a smooth paste with a little of the water and add the remaining water.
5 Add Bisto liquid and parsley to rabbit. Season. Cover and simmer for one hour.
6 Add sausages and simmer for further 10 minutes.
   Serve with creamed potatoes.

Jugged Rabbit

4 rabbit joints
4 level tsp Bisto
2 level tbsp plain flour
2oz (50g) butter or margarine
4oz (100 to 125g) streaky bacon, cut into ½ inch (1¼cm) pieces
8oz (225g) small onions or shallots
½pt (275ml) water
½pt (275ml) red wine
1 level tsp mixed herbs
2 slightly rounded tbsp redcurrant jelly

Topping
3oz (75g) fresh white breadcrumbs
1½oz (40g) butter
finely grated peel of a medium lemon

1 Wash rabbit joints and dry with paper towels. Coat with Bisto mixed with the flour.
2 Heat butter or margarine in saucepan. Add rabbit. Fry until golden all over. Remove to heavy casserole.
3 Add bacon and onions or shallots to remaining butter or margarine in pan. Fry gently for 5 minutes.
4 Stir in any remaining Bisto and flour mixture, then add water, wine, herbs and redcurrant jelly. Slowly cook till mixture bubbles and thickens.

5 Pour into casserole over rabbit. Cover. Cook 2 hours in oven set to 325°F (160°C), Gas 3.
6 For topping, fry crumbs in butter till light golden. Stir in lemon peel. Sprinkle over casserole.
   Serve hot with potatoes and green vegetables.

Venison Casserole (serves 4)

A marvellous dish to make in those areas where venison is readily available.

1 large onion, chopped
2 tbsp salad oil
1lb (500g) stewing venison, cubed
1 level tbsp flour
8oz (225g) medium-sized potatoes, quartered
4 heaped tsp Bisto
¾pt (425ml) water
¼pt (150ml) dry red wine
1 rounded tbsp redcurrant jelly
finely grated peel and juice of 1 medium orange
salt and pepper to taste

1 Fry the onion in oil for 3 minutes.
2 Toss the venison in flour and fry with the onion until lightly browned on all sides. Put into a casserole with the potatoes.
3 Blend the Bisto to a smooth paste with a little of the water. Add the remaining water.
4 Mix with the wine, redcurrant jelly, orange peel and juice, and pour over the venison. Season.
5 Cover the casserole and cook for 1½ hours at 325°F (160°C), Gas 3.
   Serve with creamed potatoes, extra redcurrant jelly and fried mushrooms.

Stewed Pigeons with Gin (serves 4)

4 cleaned pigeons, halved
2 level tbsp flour mixed with 1½ level tbsp Onion Bisto
1½oz (40g) butter
1 tbsp salad oil
3oz (75g) unsmoked back bacon, chopped
1pt (575ml) water
1 level tsp celery salt
4oz (125g) trimmed button mushrooms
3 tbsp gin

1 Coat pigeon halves with flour and Bisto mixture. Heat butter and oil in flameproof casserole.
2 Add pigeon halves, two at a time. Fry until crisp and golden-brown all over. Remove to plate.
3 Add bacon to remaining butter and oil in pan. Fry for 5 minutes. Add water and celery salt. Bring to boil.
4 Replace pigeons. Simmer, covered, about ¾ to 1 hour or till tender. Stir in mushrooms and gin.
5 Continue to simmer for a further 10 minutes.
   Serve with creamed potatoes and green vegetables.

6 Kidneys, Liver, Tongue and Tripe

Devilled Kidneys (serves 4)

Follow recipe for chicken in devilled sauce (page 99) but substitute 1lb (500g) sliced ox kidney for the chicken. Allow an extra ¼ hour cooking time.

Kidneys Braised in Red Wine (serves 4)

1lb (500g) ox kidney, cut into ½ inch (1¼cm) cubes
1oz (25g) flour
2 level tsp Onion Bisto
1oz (25g) butter or margarine
2 tsp salad oil
1 medium garlic clove, crushed
¼pt (150ml) water
¼pt (150ml) dry red wine
salt and pepper to taste
4oz (100 to 125g) button mushrooms

1 Wash kidney and wipe dry with paper towels. Toss in flour mixed with Onion Bisto.
2 Heat butter or margarine and oil in pan. Add garlic and kidney. Fry about 5 to 6 minutes or till well-sealed and golden.
3 Blend in water and wine. Bring to boil, stirring. Season. Lower heat and cover. Simmer 1 hour or till kidney is tender. Stir occasionally.
4 Add mushrooms. Continue to cook a further ¼ hour.

Serve with creamed potatoes and green vegetables to taste.

Kidney and Bacon Hotpot (serves 4)

1oz (25g) lard or dripping
1 large onion, chopped
4oz (100 to 125g) bacon pieces, chopped
1½lb (750g) pig's kidneys, well-washed, cored and diced
4 heaped tsp Bisto
¾pt (425ml) water
1 can (14oz or 400g) tomatoes
4oz (100 to 125g) trimmed mushrooms, sliced
few sprigs of parsley

1 Melt fat in pan. Add onion and bacon and fry until lightly browned.
2 Add kidney to pan and fry for a further 3 minutes.
3 Place kidney, onion and bacon in casserole.
4 Mix Bisto to a smooth paste with a little of the cold water. Blend in remaining water and pour into casserole over ingredients.
5 Cover and cook at 350°F (180°C), Gas 4, for 30 minutes.
6 Add tomatoes and mushrooms and cook for a further 15 minutes.
7 Garnish with parsley.

Serve with rice or pasta. Accompany with green vegetables.

Kidneys braised in red wine

Stuffed Savoury Hearts (serves 4)

5 tbsp boiling water
3 rounded tbsp sage-and-onion stuffing mix
4 lamb's hearts
1oz (25g) flour
3 tbsp salad oil
1 medium onion, sliced
4oz (125g) carrots, sliced
4 medium celery stalks, chopped
2 level tsp mixed herbs
3 rounded tsp Bisto
1pt (575ml) water
salt and pepper to taste

1 Add water to stuffing mix, stir and leave to stand 10 minutes.
2 Wash hearts, remove tubes, gristle and fat. Wash and dry. Cut through centre dividing tissue to make room for stuffing.
3 Stuff the hearts and tie up with string.
4 Coat the hearts with flour and fry in oil until browned on all sides. Drain and place in casserole.
5 Fry onion, carrots and celery lightly in remaining oil. Add to casserole with herbs.
6 Mix Bisto to a paste with a little of the water. Blend in remaining water, and pour over hearts and vegetables. Season to taste.
7 Cover casserole and cook 1¾ to 2 hours in oven set to 350°F (180°C), Gas 4.

Serve with creamed potatoes, green vegetables to taste and redcurrant or cranberry jelly.

Oxtail Stew (serves 4 to 6)

3lb (1½kg) cut-up oxtail
1oz (25g) margarine or dripping
2 tsp salad oil
1 large carrot, onion and parsnip, diced
1 small turnip, diced
bouquet garni
¾pt (425ml) water
1 level tsp salt
1oz (25g) plain flour, mixed with 3 rounded tsp Bisto
4 tbsp extra cold water
1 tbsp malt vinegar
2 tbsp tomato purée
salt and pepper to taste
2 level tbsp chopped parsley for garnish

1 Trim oxtail of excess fat. Wash and dry each piece thoroughly.
2 Heat fat and oil in large pan. Add oxtail. Fry briskly until well-sealed and golden. Remove to plate temporarily.
3 Add vegetables to remaining fat and oil in pan. Fry gently until golden, allowing about 20 minutes.
4 Replace oxtail. Add bouquet garni, water and salt. Bring to boil. Skim. Lower heat. Cover. Simmer 2½ to 3 hours or until oxtail is tender.
5 Leave in the cold, covered, overnight. Remove hard layer of fat from the top. To thicken, put flour and Bisto into bowl. Mix smoothly with water and vinegar. Add purée.
6 Bring pan of oxtail to the boil. Trickle in flour mixture, stirring continuously till gravy thickens. Boil 3 minutes.
7 Adjust seasoning to taste, spoon into a serving dish and sprinkle with parsley.

Accompany with boiled potatoes and mixed vegetables.

Oxtail Stew with Wine (serves 4 to 6)
Substitute dry red wine for the ¾pt (425ml) water.

Farmhouse chicken stew

Boiled Tongue (serves 10 to 12)

1 fresh or brined ox tongue (weighing about 5lb or
  2¼kg)
cold water
8 cloves
1lb (500g) onions, peeled but left whole
8oz (225g) carrots, peeled but left whole
2 large celery stalks, broken into threes
1 bay leaf
bouquet garni

1 Trim tongue, removing unwanted fat from root
end.
2 Put into large pan. Cover with cold water. Bring
slowly to boil. Drain. Cover with more fresh water.
3 Bring to boil. Lower heat. Cover. Simmer 5 hours,
when tongue should be tender. Add cloves,
vegetables, bay leaf and bouquet garni half-way
through.
4 Drain. Leave to cool off slightly. Strip off skin.
Remove bones, gristle and fat from root end. Discard.

Carve into slices and serve hot with gravy made
from Bisto Rich Gravy Granules. Accompany with
boiled potatoes and green vegetables to taste.

Tongue with Sherry Sauce (serves 10 to 12)

Cook tongue as directed in recipe for boiled tongue,
above. Serve with 1pt (575ml) gravy made from Bisto
Rich Gravy Granules to which 2 or 3 tbsp dry sherry
has been added. Reheat till hot.

Tongue with Madeira Sauce (serves 10 to 12)

A classic dish, simplified by using Bisto gravy
granules. Make up 1pt (575ml) gravy using the gravy
granules as directed. Stir in 3 level tbsp tomato purée,
3 tbsp Madeira and a pinch of powdered bay leaves
(omit if not easily available). Reheat until bubbling
gently. Serve with the sliced tongue.

Tongue with Onion and Horseradish Sauce (serves 10 to 12)

Cook tongue as directed in recipe for boiled tongue.
Serve with 1pt (575ml) gravy made from Bisto Rich
Gravy Granules to which has been added 1 chopped
and butter-fried medium onion and 1 tbsp
horseradish relish.

Swiss Liver Skewers (serves 4)

1lb (500g) chicken livers, washed and dried
lemon juice
1 level tsp dried sage
4 long rashers streaky bacon, derinded
2oz (50g) butter or margarine
3 rounded tsp Bisto
¼pt (150ml) water
3 tbsp dry red wine
salt and pepper to taste

1 Thread livers on to 4 large skewers. Sprinkle with
lemon juice. Dust with sage. Wind a bacon rasher,
spiral fashion, round each skewer over liver.
2 Melt butter or margarine in large pan. Add liver
skewers. Fry gently about 20 minutes, carefully
turning each one twice.
3 Remove to warm serving dish and keep hot. Stir
Bisto into remaining fat in pan. Gradually blend in
water and wine. Season.
4 Cook, stirring, until mixture comes to boil and
thickens. Serve as gravy with the liver.

Accompany with creamed potatoes and green
vegetables.

Italian Liver with Sage (serves 4)

1lb (500g) pork liver, cut into 4 slices
4 level tsp Onion Bisto, mixed with 1 level tsp dried
  sage
2oz (50g) butter
2 tsp salad oil
4 tbsp Marsala
salt and pepper to taste

1 Wash and dry liver. Coat each piece with Bisto and
sage mixture.
2 Heat butter and oil in frying pan till hot. Add liver.
Fry about 8 to 10 minutes or until cooked through,
turning twice.
3 Transfer to serving dish. Add Marsala to pan. Heat
until bubbly and reduced by about one third. Season.
Pour over liver.
4 Serve with sauté potatoes and buttered leaf spinach
or other green vegetables to taste.

Liver and Macaroni Casserole (serves 4)

1lb (500g) lamb's liver
1lb (500g) onions, sliced
3 tbsp salad oil
½ level tsp mixed herbs
3 rounded tsp Bisto
1¼pt (about ¾ litre) water
3oz (75g) elbow macaroni or pasta shells
salt and pepper to taste

1 Wash and trim the liver. Cut into thin strips.
2 Fry onions lightly in oil for 4 minutes. Drain and
transfer to casserole.
3 Brown liver in remaining oil and transfer to
casserole.
4 Add herbs. Mix Bisto to a smooth paste with a little
of the water. Blend in remaining water and pour into
casserole.
5 Cover and cook for 40 minutes at 350°F (180°C),
Gas 4.
6 Remove casserole from oven and add macaroni or
shells. Adjust seasoning to taste.

7 Return casserole to oven and cook for a further 15 to 20 minutes until macaroni or shells are tender.

Chicken Livers Plaza (serves 4 to 5)

Not unlike the creamed turkey Veronique on page 102, this is a rather splendid liver dish that is worth considering for a dinner party or important celebratory meal. To make the dish in party style, double up on all the ingredients.

1lb (500g) chicken livers in tubs, thawed if frozen
1 level tbsp flour, mixed with 3 heaped tsp Bisto
1oz (25g) butter
2 tsp salad oil
1 medium onion, chopped
2 tbsp dry sherry
5 tbsp water
3 tbsp thick mayonnaise
3 heaped tbsp soured cream
salt and pepper to taste
¼ level tsp sage

1 Wash and dry livers. Toss in flour and Bisto mixture, making sure all pieces are coated.
2 Heat butter and oil in shallow pan. Add liver. Fry until golden-brown and crisp on both sides. Remove to dish temporarily.
3 Add onion to remaining butter and oil in pan. Fry until pale gold and soft. Keep heat low and pan covered. Allow about ¼ hour.
4 Stir in sherry and water, then replace livers. Simmer about 20 minutes, adding extra boiling water if sauce seems to be thickening too much.
5 Add mayonnaise and cream, season to taste, stir in sage and reheat without boiling.
   Serve with creamed potatoes and tiny peas.

Chicken Livers Creole (serves 6)

Follow recipe for bacon chops creole (page 77), but use chicken livers instead of bacon chops. Rinse and drain the livers and fry in butter or margarine until cooked through.

Liver in Madeira Sauce (serves 4)

1 medium onion, chopped
1oz (25g) butter
1 tsp salad oil
1lb (500g) lamb's liver, cubed (all gristle removed)
2 level tsp cornflour
2 level tsp Bisto
2 level tsp mild curry powder
large pinch cayenne pepper
juice of 1 large orange
5 tbsp Madeira (or port)
¼pt (150ml) water
salt and pepper to taste
1 sliced orange for garnishing

1 Fry onion in butter and oil until light gold. Add liver. Fry a little more briskly until all pieces are well-sealed and brown.
2 Stir in cornflour, Bisto, curry and cayenne pepper. Cook 2 minutes.
3 Add all remaining ingredients. Bring to boil, stirring continuously.
4 Lower heat and cover. Simmer gently 20 minutes. Transfer to warm serving dish and garnish with orange slices.
   Accompany with rice and green vegetables.

Florence Tripe (serves 6)

Make up the luxury Bolognese sauce as directed on page 28. Cook 2lb (1kg) dressed tripe for about ½ to ¾ hour or until tender. Drain thoroughly. Cut into strips or squares. Heat through till piping hot in the Bolognese sauce.
   Serve with rice or macaroni. Top each portion with grated Parmesan cheese.

Italian Tripe (serves 4)

1½lb (750g) dressed tripe, cut into small squares or
   strips
1 large onion, sliced
1 large garlic clove, crushed
2 tbsp salad oil
1 medium green pepper, de-seeded and cut into strips
1 small can (8oz or 225g) tomatoes
1 rounded tbsp tomato purée
salt and pepper to taste
2 rounded tsp Bisto
¼pt (150ml) water

1 Boil tripe in salted water for 10 minutes and drain.
2 Fry the onion and garlic for 4 minutes in the oil.
3 Add the green pepper and cook for a further 3 minutes.
4 Stir in the tomatoes, tomato purée, seasoning and Bisto mixed smoothly with the water.
5 Add the drained tripe and simmer, covered, for 45 minutes.
   Serve with cooked pasta or rice.

Mixed grill

French-style Tripe and Onions (serves 4)

2lb (1kg) dressed tripe
2oz (50g) butter or margarine
8oz (225g) onions, chopped
2 level tbsp flour
3 rounded tsp Bisto
¾pt (425ml) water
salt and pepper to taste

1 Wash tripe thoroughly, wipe dry on paper towels and cut into 2 inch (5cm) squares.
2 Heat butter or margarine in large pan. Add onions. Fry gently until deep golden, allowing about 20 minutes.
3 Add tripe and fry till lightly browned, turning often.
4 Stir in flour and Bisto, then gradually add water. Cook, stirring all the time, until sauce comes to the boil and thickens. Season.
5 Lower heat and cover. Simmer gently for ¾ hour or until tripe is tender. Stir occasionally to prevent sticking.

Serve with freshly cooked pasta or creamed potatoes. Sprouts or cabbage team well with the tripe.

7 Mixed Meat Dishes; Accompaniments

Lamb and Kidney Ragout (serves 4)

1½lb (750g) middle neck of lamb, cut into small
   pieces
6oz (175g) pig's kidneys, cored and cut into small
   cubes
1oz (25g) flour, seasoned with salt and pepper
3 tbsp salad oil
2 level tbsp tomato purée
1 large onion, grated
4 rounded tsp Bisto
1pt (575ml) water
3 medium carrots, sliced

1 Dust the lamb and kidney with flour. Fry in the oil
until browned on all sides.
2 Add the tomato purée and the grated onion.
3 Blend the Bisto to a smooth paste with a little of the
water. Mix with the remaining water.
4 Add the Bisto liquid to the meat and bring to the
boil.
5 Put into a casserole with the sliced carrots. Cover
the casserole and cook for 2 hours at 325°F (160°C),
Gas 3.

Mixed Grill (serves 4)

2 lamb's kidneys
4oz (100 to 125g) button mushrooms
1oz (25g) butter or margarine
2 tomatoes, halved
12oz (350g) rump steak, cut into 4 pieces
4 rashers streaky bacon, de-rinded
4 pork chipolata sausages
watercress

1 Skin kidneys, then cut in half and remove central
cores and fat. Trim mushrooms. Wash if necessary
and wipe dry with paper towels.
2 Heat butter or margarine in grill pan. Add kidneys,
mushrooms and tomatoes, turning in the hot fat till
evenly coated. Grill 5 minutes, turning once.
3 Remove grill pan from heat. Add pieces of steak.
Halve bacon rashers widthwise and roll up. Stand in
grill pan with sausages.
4 Grill all the ingredients a further 4 minutes. Turn
over. Grill 4 to 5 minutes or till cooked to taste.

5 Arrange on a warm dish and garnish with
watercress.
   Serve with fried potatoes or chips, peas, and Bisto
gravy made from Bisto Rich Gravy Granules and
boiling water as directed.

Tip
To make a thriftier mixed grill, substitute lamb
cutlets or hamburgers for the rump steak.

Italian Fritto Misto (serves 8)

This is a filling and typically Italian dish, and well
worth making if you're keen on informal entertaining
and are having a gathering of friends around you in
the kitchen. The fritto misto is best served piping hot
from the pan and does not travel well even to the
dining room!

8oz (225g) chicken livers, cut up into cubes
8oz (225g) piece of leg of veal, cubed
8oz (225g) feather blade steak, cubed
½ small head of cauliflower, parboiled and divided
   into florets
6oz (175g) button mushrooms
salt and pepper

Batter
4oz (100 to 125g) plain flour
3 level tsp Onion Bisto
1 × Grade 2 (large) egg
2 tsp salad oil
¼pt (150ml) water
salt and pepper to taste

For frying
salad oil

1 Sprinkle livers, veal, steak, cauliflower and
mushrooms with salt and pepper. Leave on one side
temporarily.
2 To make batter, sift flour and Bisto into bowl. Beat
to a thick, smooth and creamy batter with egg, oil and
water. Season to taste with salt and pepper.
3 Dip all prepared ingredients into the batter. Lift
out and fry in deep hot oil until crisp, golden and
cooked through.
4 Drain on paper towels and serve very hot with
wedges of lemon and a mixed salad. Crusty bread
makes a substantial accompaniment.

Italian fritto misto

Cassoulet (serves 6)

A hearty dish from France which makes excellent winter eating.

6oz (175g) butter beans, soaked overnight and parboiled in unsalted water
8oz (225g) breast of lamb, boned
12oz (350g) blade of pork, boned
6oz (175g) garlic sausage (buy a small chubby one)
1½oz (40g) margarine
3 level tsp Bisto
4oz (100 to 125g) streaky bacon, chopped
2 large onions, sliced
1 bouquet garni
1½pt (just under 1 litre) water
6 × 1 inch (2½cm) slices day-old French bread
oil

1 Drain parboiled butter beans and leave on one side for the time being.
2 Remove and discard excess fat from lamb and pork. Cut meat into 1 inch (2½cm) cubes. Skin and slice sausage fairly thickly.
3 Heat margarine in large pan. Add meats and sausage slices. Fry until lightly browned. Stir in Bisto.
4 Fill an ovenproof dish with layers of beans, fried meats and sausage, the chopped bacon and onions. Add bouquet garni.
5 Pour in water, cover with lid and cook for 2½ to 3 hours in cool oven set to 300°F (150°C), Gas 2. Remove cassoulet from oven and uncover.
6 Top with bread slices dipped in oil. Return to oven for a further ½ hour.

To serve, put a bread slice on to 6 warm plates and add spoons of cassoulet. Eat while still very hot.

Serbian Mixed Meat Hotpot (serves 4 to 6)

Slightly oriental in character, the hotpot is worth making in early autumn when all the vegetables are at their very best.

2lb (1kg) skinned tomatoes, chopped
1 medium washed and dried aubergine, coarsely chopped
2 medium green peppers, de-seeded and cut into strips
1lb (500g) trimmed courgettes, thinly sliced
1lb (500g) onions, very thinly sliced
3 heaped tsp Bisto
4 tbsp salad oil
1lb (500g) chuck steak, diced
1lb (500g) hand of pork (boned weight), diced
2oz (50g) short grain pudding rice
½pt (275ml) water

1 Put all the vegetables into a large bowl and toss with Bisto and oil. Arrange half the mixture in *large* casserole. Top with both meats.
2 Sprinkle with rice. Pour water into dish. Top with remaining vegetable mixture. Cover with lid or foil.
3 Cook in 2½ to 3 hours in oven set to 325°F (160°C), Gas 3.

Spoon onto plates and serve with boiled potatoes.

Yugoslav Djuvec (serves 4)

8oz (225g) pork fillet
8oz (225g) rump skirt
8oz (225g) onions
2 small aubergines, washed but unskinned
3 medium green peppers, halved and de-seeded
3 tbsp salad oil
4oz (125g) long-grain rice
2 level tsp Bisto

¾pt (425ml) water
½ level tsp marjoram
1lb (500g) skinned tomatoes, chopped

1 Cut meat into strips. Cut onions into wafer-thin slices. Dice aubergines. Cut green peppers into thin shreds.
2 Heat oil in pan. Add meat, a few pieces at a time, and fry briskly until golden and crisp all over. Remove to plate. Add vegetables to rest of oil. Fry gently for ¼ hour. Replace meat. Add rice.
3 Mix Bisto smoothly with a little of the water. Add rest of water. Pour into pan. Simmer ½ hour, covered. Stir occasionally.
4 Stir in marjoram and tomatoes. Continue to cook a further 10 minutes.
   Serve with salad.

Scandinavian Frikadeller (serves 6 to 8)

Well-appreciated throughout Denmark, Norway, Finland and Sweden, these tasty meat balls are a delicious and economical way of using minced beef or pork—or sometimes a combination. They team best with boiled potatoes and cranberry sauce, and the most appropriate vegetable is red cabbage in the winter and baby carrots, mixed with peas and beans, in the summer. The frikadeller can be eaten hot or cold.

1lb (500g) lean, raw minced beef
8oz (225g) lean, raw minced pork
1 large onion, finely grated
3 level tsp Bisto
½ level tsp mixed spice
4oz (100 to 125g) fresh white breadcrumbs
1 × Grade 2 (large) egg, beaten
¼pt (150ml) evaporated milk, undiluted
salt and pepper to taste
fat for frying

1 Mix beef and pork with all remaining ingredients except fat.
2 When thoroughly combined, shape into about 16 × 1 inch (2½cm) ovals. Use damp hands to prevent the meat mixture from becoming sticky.
3 Fry, a few at a time, in hot fat till golden-brown on both sides and cooked through. Allow about 5 to 6 minutes.
4 Drain on paper towels and serve with suggested accompaniments.

Note
If preferred, all beef may be used and the pork omitted.

Scandinavian Cocktail Frikadeller (serves 8 to 10)

Follow above recipe but shape mixture into balls slightly larger than walnuts. Fry in hot fat and drain. Spear with cocktail sticks and serve hot or cold.

Red cabbage (serves 8)
3lb (1½kg) red cabbage, finely shredded
2 heaped tsp Bisto
1 level tbsp cornflour
¾pt (350ml) water
1 large onion, grated
2 large Bramley apples, peeled, cored and sliced
5 tbsp mild vinegar
2 level tbsp soft brown sugar
1 to 2 level tsp salt
2 to 3 cloves

1 Put cabbage into a large and heavy-based pan. Mix Bisto and cornflour together. Blend in water to form thin paste.
2 Add to cabbage with all remaining ingredients. Bring to a gentle bubble, stirring continuously. Simmer 2 hours, stirring from time to time to prevent sticking.
3 Cool. Leave 24 hours before reheating and serving, as the flavour will mature and develop if allowed to rest.

Salzburg Almond Sauce (serves 6)

A somewhat extravagant luxury, but highly recommended for all game dishes, freshly cooked and sliced smoked tongue and grilled or fried gammon rashers.

2oz (50g) butter or margarine
2 tsp salad oil
6oz (175g) onions, finely chopped
6oz (175g) Bramley apples, peeled and chopped
1 rounded tsp flour
3 rounded tsp Bisto
½pt (275ml) water
4 tbsp dry white wine
4 inch (10cm) strip of lemon peel
pinch powdered cloves
salt and pepper to taste
2oz (50g) blanched and coarsely chopped almonds, toasted till light gold
2 level tsp caster sugar
2oz (50g) green grapes, halved and with pips removed

1 Heat butter or margarine and oil in deepish frying pan till foamy. Add onions and apples. Fry until pale gold, stirring from time to time.
2 Work in flour and Bisto. Gradually blend in water and wine. Cook, stirring, until sauce comes to boil and thickens.
3 Add lemon peel, cloves and seasoning. Cover. Bubble gently for ¼ hour. Take out lemon peel. Add rest of ingredients. Stir well to mix.
Serve hot.

Potato Pancakes (serves 6)

1½lb (750g) raw potatoes, peeled and grated
3oz (75g) onion, grated
2 rounded tbsp plain flour
2 × Grade 2 (large) eggs, beaten
salt and pepper to taste
salad oil for frying

1 Place potatoes and onion into bowl. Add all remaining ingredients except oil. Mix well. Cover. Leave to stand ½ hour. Mixture will turn a muddy colour but this is satisfactory.
2 Heat approximately 1 inch (2½cm) oil in frying pan. Drop a heaped tbsp potato mixture into hot oil. Flatten slightly with back of a spoon.
3 Fry until golden-brown and crisp on both sides, turning twice. Remove from pan. Drain on paper towels. Repeat until all the mixture is used up.
Serve hot with boiled salted beef, or as you choose.

Suet Dumplings (serves 6 to 8)

8oz (225g) self-raising flour
1 level tsp salt
4oz (125g) finely shredded suet
about 6 tbsp cold water to mix

1 Sift flour and salt into bowl. Toss in suet. Mix to a fairly stiff dough with water.
2 Turn out on to floured surface. Knead lightly until smooth. Divide into 8 pieces.
3 Roll into smooth balls with floured hands. Drop into pan of boiling salted water.
4 Simmer, uncovered, about ¼ hour. Remove from pan with perforated spoon. Serve with boiled salted beef or stews.

Cassoulet

Freezing Meat

First of all ask your local butcher about buying meat in quantity for your freezer. Think carefully about buying whole or part of a carcase, as many cuts of meat are included which you may not normally buy. The butcher can buy meat in quantity and he will cut and pack the required amount for you. If you place a regular order he should offer you a discount.

Often frozen meat specialists are the next best source: the meat is supplied in individual joints or selection packs containing a variety of cuts. The preparation and initial freezing are complete before buying, ensuring that the meat is quickly frozen in peak condition.

Bulk buying suppliers do not usually specialise in meat, so check carefully the quantity and quality offered for the price quoted. Particular care must be taken when buying selection packs as the overall price may be misleading.

Preparation for Freezing

Rapid freezing is most important. Always set the freezer control to the coldest setting or set to 'fast freeze' for several hours beforehand and leave until meat is frozen; then return to normal setting. The quicker meat is frozen the better the quality and condition of it during storage.

Allow one cubic foot of freezer space to every 2lb to 3lb (1 to 1½kg) meat to be frozen. Cleanliness is essential: good quality moisture and vapour-proof materials should be used for packaging fresh meat: for example, freezer foil and heavy duty polythene bags are ideal. Separate chops, steak or chicken portions with plastic film wrap for easy separation, and cut stewing steak into small pieces for quick thawing. Protect bones with extra packing; boneless joints take up less room in the freezer.

Pack poultry in the normal way, then place in a box surrounded with packing and place in freezer. This prevents the awkward shape becoming damaged during storage.

Exclude all air, seal bags with freezer tape or wire tags, label clearly giving date, weight and cut of meat. Store meat and poultry for up to nine months.

To Thaw

All meat must be completely thawed before cooking to obtain the best results. Thaw slowly, by placing meat in the refrigerator for up to 24 hours. Allow 5-6 hours per pound (500g) of meat. Don't forget to defrost your freezer regularly to keep all food in peak condition.

Meat Cooking Terms

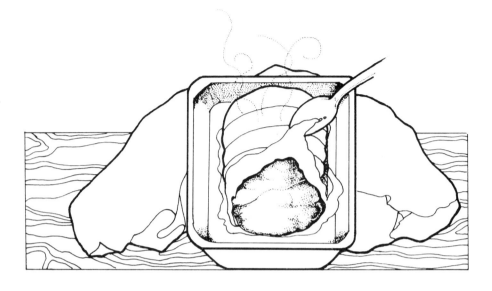

Barding
Covering wings and breasts of poultry and game birds with thin pieces of bacon to prevent scorching and dryness.

Basting
Coating joints of meat and poultry, etc, with the pan juices while they are roasting. This is usually done with a spoon at regular intervals, about every 20 to 30 minutes depending on the length of cooking time. Basting helps to keep flesh moist and, to some extent, prevents shrinkage. It also improves appearance.

Beating
Flattening meat, breaking down the fibrous tissue in order to tenderise it. This may be done at home with a rolling pin or mallet. Butchers now use a special machine to produce 'flash-fry' steaks, hence the rough texture.

Boiling
Cooking food in a liquid at a temperature of 212°F or 100°C. Although meat, etc, is often described as boiled, it is more generally simmered in water that is kept literally trembling without bubbling. Rapid and consistent boiling of meat would cause unnecessary shrinkage and also spoil colour, flavour and texture.

Braising
Part-cooking meat or poultry in a flameproof casserole on top of the stove, and then transferring it to the oven to finish off. It is usual to line the casserole with assorted vegetables and also add some sort of liquid—stock, water, wine, cider or beer.

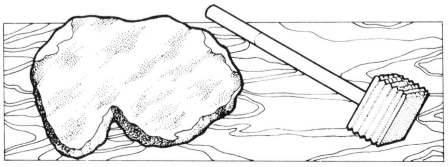

Roast turkey

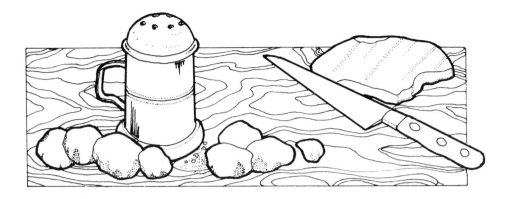

Brining

Meat (usually pork, beef or offal) is brined by being left soaking in a brine solution made from specified amounts of salt and water. The length of time to brine the meat depends on the recipe instructions.

Broiling

American term for conventional grilling.

Casseroling

To cook meat, poultry, offal, etc, with vegetables and liquid, in a heatproof casserole dish in the oven. To avoid evaporation, the lid should be a good fit. If not, a close cover of foil is more reliable.

En Croîte

Cooking meat *en croîte* is to wrap it in a complete 'overcoat' of pastry, well sealed.

Dredging

Sprinkling pieces of meat, etc, for frying with flour or cornflour; most easily done with a flour dredger (like a sifter with holes).

Frying—Deep Fat

Cooking flour-dredged, egg-and-crumbed or batter-coated pieces of meat, offal or poultry in a *deep* pan half-filled with hot oil or fat. Only a few pieces should be placed in the pan at once and they should be fully immersed. If too many were added at once, the temperature of the oil or fat would fall and in consequence the food would be greasy and soggy. Fried food must be well-drained on kitchen paper.

Frying—Shallow Fat

Cooking in a small amount of fat in a shallow pan. This is suitable for slim slices of meat and offal, also chops.

Grilling

Cooking tender cuts of meat, etc, relatively quickly under direct (radiant) heat coming from gas or electricity. Also browning pre-cooked dishes, or those with cheese or crumb topping, briefly under a high heat. The grill should always be pre-heated to ensure satisfactory results and prevent toughness.

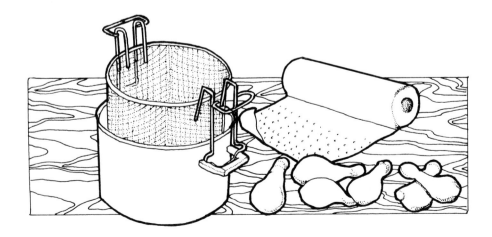

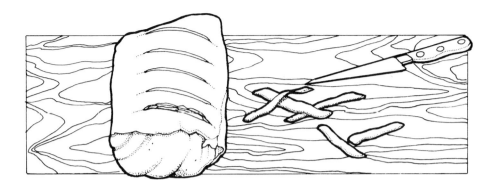

Larding
Making cuts in joints of meat and filling them with pieces of fat bacon or pork fat. The object is to keep the meat moist and flavoursome. Professionals use a larding needle specially designed for the purpose.

Marinating
Soaking (or marinating) meat, poultry, offal or game in a mixture of oil with wine, cider, vinegar or lemon juice, seasonings, spices and herbs. It is a technique which improves flavour and helps to tenderise the flesh.

En Papillote
Cooking pieces of meat, poultry or offal *en papillote* means wrapping them in greased greaseproof paper or foil. The wrapping should be split open and folded back before the meat is served.

Poaching
Cooking some white meat and poultry dishes (and offal such as sweetbreads) *very gently* in sufficient liquid—usually milk or water or a combination of the two—to cover. The pan is usually left uncovered.

Pot Roasting
'Roasting' on top of the cooker in a saucepan with a well-fitting lid. A little fat (or oil) to taste is usually added. This method is particularly recommended for small and/or tougher portions of meat.

Reducing
Boiling down meat or poultry juices, *after* the food has been cooked, in order to produce a concentrated liquid, a half or a third of its original volume. The liquid is then used to make a sauce or gravy.

Roasting
Cooking meat and poultry, etc, in the dry heat of an oven, by means of convection and radiation. It is a method of cooking best suited to tender cuts and young birds.

Scalding
Covering meat, etc, with boiling water in order to remove animal hairs more easily, and also to cleanse the flesh.

Simmering
Cooking in a liquid kept below boiling point. (See Boiling.)

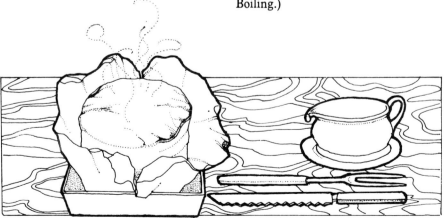

Steaming

Cooking delicate cuts of light meats and poultry in a deep plate or bowl over gently simmering water. The food should be well seasoned and the plate or bowl kept covered. As no fat need be added, it is a useful method of cooking for those who are on low-fat diets or have digestive disorders.

Stewing

Simmering meat, etc, or meat and vegetables, in a pan with a well-fitting lid.

'If a stew boils, a stew spoils' is a good piece of old-fashioned advice; a stew should never be allowed to bubble vigorously. A gentle simmer is best for the tougher cuts of meat which require long, slow cooking.

Thickening

Adding flour or cornflour to cooking liquid in order to thicken it. Depending on the recipe, this can be done at the beginning—when cubes of meat, etc, are coated with the thickening agent—or at the very end, when the flour or cornflour is combined with cold liquid and added to the meat and poultry mixture. Thickening at the end helps to eliminate sticking and burning, especially if a dish has to cook for a very long time.

Stuffed pork roll

Index